Fireflies In A Fruit Jar

On Religion, Politics, And Other Wonders
By A Southern Preacher-Turned- Journalist

AUGUST HOUSE

Fireflies In A Fruit Jar

On Religion, Politics, And Other Wonders
By A Southern Preacher-Turned-Journalist

John S. Workman

With Sally Chandler Crisp

August House / Little Rock
PUBLISHERS

Printed in the United States of America

10 9 8 7 6 5 4

LIBRARY OF CONGRESS CATALOGING-IN-PUBLICATION DATA

Workman, John S., 1927-
Fireflies in a fruit jar: on religion, politics, and other
wonders by a southern preacher-turned-journalist /
John S. Workman, with Sally Crisp. — 1st ed.

   p.   cm.
ISBN 0-87483-053-2 (pbk. : alk. paper) : $9.95
1. Meditations.   I. Crisp, Sally.   II. Title.
BV4832.2.W68 1988   87-28991
    242—dc 19   CIP

Cover design by Bill Jennings
Production artwork by Ira Hocut
Typography by Diversitype, Inc.
Design direction by Ted Parkhurst
Project direction by Hope Coulter

This book is printed on archival-quality paper which
meets the guidelines for performance and durability of
the Committee on Production Guidelines for Book Lon-
gevity of the Council on Library Resources.

AUGUST HOUSE, INC. PUBLISHERS LITTLE ROCK

To my wife, Liz, and our children,
John, Steve, Susie, and Chuck.

Thanks.

Acknowledgments

With unending gratitude to all those who—though often with "blinking" lights—use their faith to help others along the way.

With equal gratitude to all those slayers of the dragons of sorrow, grief, illness, and pain. Thank you for your example.

Go forth, little fireflies of God. Let your lights shine.

JSW

For all you have given and continue to give, my love and gratitude to Huey, Molly, and Mitchell, my partners in keeping on keeping on, and to Lucille Chandler Bryson, my first and always faith teacher; for care and devotion in this project and for friendship, to Sandie Jacobi, and for assistance with the manuscript, to Barry Maid and to Carla Daniels; for support with my research, to the many nice folks at the *Arkansas Gazette*, particularly Martha Tanner; for friendship and for fruit jars, to Ted and Liz Parkhurst ... and, of course, to John Workman—for trust and for fireflies.

SCC

Contents

Foreword

John Workman runs deep, like a powerful river that can carry the freight. When John sits in a meeting, he's quiet—a listener, a thinker. But when he picks up his pen or pounds his typewriter, sparks begin to fly.

The man can write! His words lilt with laughter, sparkle with erudite insights, and gently press home the point. His country-style Arkansas expressions are the sugar that helps the medicine go down.

Whoever heard of a trained theologian and minister writing the religious news in the secular press? Or, to put it another way, when was a journalist so perceptive of the gospel's deepest meanings? What a bridge, what a long-spanned bridge, John Workman is across the chasm between the everyday workaday world and the church of God.

Every Saturday morning I hurry to get the paper. I forget the comics and the sports for a moment, and plunge headlong into the Workman column. I loved what he wrote about the TV evangelists. Not too hard, not judgmental, just aware of sin wherever it's found. And quick to look right at home, right in our own churches at our own sins.

He wrote: "The bad deeds of the few are reflecting on the many. Legitimate religion is being tarred with the same brush applied to the Elmer Gantrys."

But watch as he turns the spotlight. "The church, of all institutions, ought not to be surprised by sin .... People *are* (pardon the word) sinners. Yep—even you nice folks who read these words and the one who writes them. Sinners all."

Suddenly I quit throwing stones and started offering prayers!

John is quick with a current phrase, writing about the TV situation with words like "Pearlygate," "Unholy War," and "War Stars." He is equally capable of using quaint expressions, surely learned in the country churches and towns of Arkansas.

With a smile he can turn the knife. "Keep your eyes on the Lord and do your work as best you can. That's it. Sermon's over. Amen. (You don't have to send money.)"

On issues of racial justice, we can count on John. When it comes to women and men being equal in the sight of God, and one in Christ Jesus, we know where Workman stands. When starving people become visible in Ethiopia and elsewhere, the column clamors for compassion. When the arms race explodes into a hot, mad dash toward destruction, John speaks out. As the administration continues to send weapons to Central America in spite of pleas from the religious community, John Workman writes as if he were touched by Archbishop Romero and the blood of the martyrs.

John has a great wife, too. Liz shows the same social conscience, the same courage to speak out on issues of justice and compassion as her articulate husband. What a team! Their commitment to Jesus Christ and the church is so deep, so profound, so total, that they inspire others, including myself, to greater fidelity.

When I read John Workman's columns I never feel quite comfortable. He stirs me up, makes me rethink my politics. Anything that smacks of hypocrisy will be harpooned. Anything phony, even covered by a pulpit gown, will be exposed. Sort of like the prophets of Israel.

But his own vulnerability, his own honesty, his own sincere appraisal is so clearly presented, we can only read and contemplate and decide for ourselves. When

John developed cancer, what did he do right off? Why, write about it, of course, and poke fun at himself with his hair falling out, and make us meditate on our own mortality.

We are privileged to have a writer like John S. Workman, week by week interpreting the news from a religious perspective. The United Methodist Church is proud to have so splendid an interpreter of the faith.

Many of us are fortunate to have as fine a friend as John S. Workman, and his wife, Liz. Every reader of this book will be twice blessed.

Richard B. Wilke

Bishop, Arkansas Area
The United Methodist Church

Introduction

Putting this book together has been something like putting fireflies in a fruit jar. For one thing, it's been firefly season, and I have done a good bit of the pursuing, wondering, and worrying over it while I sat in my back porch swing, under the morning glory vines, 'til the fireflies came out. For another thing, I've had a rather child-like awe these several weeks at having these words, these sentences, these bits of light from a writer I admire "belong" to me, shed light for me ...

From his rectangle at the top of the *Arkansas Gazette*'s religion page, smiling a curious smile from his picture in the corner, John Workman has given us himself—in lessons, memories, dreams, laughs, questions, encouragements, stories, visions, sermons—and all for the price of the Saturday morning paper. It has been worth much more.

John Workman has been for those of us in his "flock" a wonder-full faith teacher. We have been reminded by his words, and by his example, that life is a wonderful, mysterious gift, and that faith, hope, and love come wrapped in the package with it. John's faith has a sense of adventure, anticipation—a sense of expectancy, a readiness for serendipity. It is advent thinking; it is Easter hope. It is joy and delight, and it is, of course, tears. But always there's the readiness for epiphany, always the will to turn the next corner, to go over the next hill, not with dread or fear, but with a child's "waiting for Christmas" excitement.

I hope this book captures something of John's faith. I

know his hope is here. (He told me recently that hope is "a priceless possession ... out *there* waiting and wanting to be discovered," but it's here, too, I know, captured for future reflection, meditation, inspiration.) And his gift of humor is here as well. Be advised: it—John's humor—has defied confinement; though you will find it concentrated in "On Hold for Dr. Bigpreacher," it radiates throughout. And his love (and loves), his delight, his joy—all are here—ready, I think, to give some light.

In a piece called "To Speak of Duty," John advised us of our duty as children of light. He said we were to "go forth and shine." John has surely practiced what he has preached. Both are here, the preaching and the practicing. Enjoy the glow.

Sally Crisp
July 1987

To Dream of Spring

It is interesting to ponder the seasons' effects upon our moods and manners. Some say the seasons have a profound influence on us ... One suspects that the seasons have more to do with the mystery of our lives than we imagine.

Spring, the Grass Grower

Contrary to the counsel of a colleague who says it's too early to write about spring (what do colleagues know?), we've held off about as long as we can. We're about to give in to that irrepressible urge, an annual ritual, and try to say something nice about the mother of the seasons. It's time again, before she makes her debut, to sing the praises of The Grand Matriarch.

No matter what the calendar may say, it's never too early—or too late—to dream of spring.

One must believe that somewhere it's always spring. Just as Professor Harold Hill of *The Music Man* believed "there'll always be a band," human beings are built to believe in spring. We are programmed, as we say in this computer age, to be the pursuers, the suitors, the wooers of spring.

Thoughts of spring can come at any season, although winter is perhaps their favorite.

Although the seasons are of a whole and by nature indivisible, they have their unique symbolism, their own message, their peculiar mystique. While what could be said about one is part of what could be said about each, it could be argued that spring is the *religious* season. She is the theologian among her brothers. She is nature's mystic, its seer, its saint.

If religion speaks of new life and new birth, so does spring. If religion tells of creation and beginnings and the promise of fulfillment, so does spring. If religion reveals beauty and splendor and inspires dreams and visions, so does spring. One could almost believe that spring offers a salvation of sorts.

Spring is not only a season. It is an attitude. It is hope and trust. It is a conviction that the universe is faithful.

As an attitude, spring cannot be confined by any boundaries. There is no subject, no person, no concern, no issue to which spring is not relevant.

Spring the attitude has bad news for any who would limit its meanings only to the lacy, lonely, gentler arenas of life.

Spring is a justice seeker, a relentless crusader, a setter of right. Spring is a grass grower. Spring has something to say about the most unlikely of subjects: minority rights, arms races, poverty, capital punishment, greed, social justice, and whatever other subjects might be at hand.

Spring marches to the beat of a Drummer who knows how things are meant to be. Spring is prophet as well as pastor and priest.

The Creator has numerous ways to accomplish the Divine plan. Spring, as season and attitude, is one such way.

It is never too early or too late or too cold or too warm to let Mother Spring work her magic.

It's Worth the Wait

No matter how long it takes to get here, spring is always worth the wait. The longer it takes, the sweeter it is.

Surely there are parables in spring's late arrival—or, as some might regard it, in winter's prolonged departure.

So long as human beings have waited for spring, or waited out the winter, there have been attempts to philosophize about the experience. It was true in the hoary past when magic and gods were credited with the mysteries attending such things, and it is true today when computers and satellites trick us into believing we can really understand the mischief of the seasons.

Father Winter and Mother Spring, in their wily ways,

outwitted our forebears and continue to do so to us today, even with all our technological wizardry.

Many of us like it that way. What an uncertain blessing it will be when we can *truly* forecast the weather. How sad to take from us this grand mystery of not really knowing what Mother Nature has in store for her children. It is good to know there are still a few mysteries that human beings haven't been able to unravel.

Such unknowns remind us that we are creature, not Creator. They remind us of our ultimate dependence on God—something a technologically sophisticated age tends to forget.

Spring and winter and summer and fall have a wisdom that surpasses all that mere mortals could ever fathom. It's infinitely good that way.

There are lessons from spring's late arrival:

■We shouldn't presume on the Creator. We shouldn't count our jonquils before they've hatched.

We checked and found that our first annual paean in praise of spring '83 came in this column way back in the middle of January, no less, when the fickle lady tempted us to believe her arrival was imminent. How foolish to fall for such flirtings, a danger that colleagues warned of at the time. (We were wiser—"What do colleagues know?")

Spring, and her Creator, have minds of their own. They don't take kindly to second-guessing.

■We should take life and all its offerings, including spring and winter, as they come—or as they don't.

There isn't any option, of course. But many of us act as if there were. We want what we want when we want it and most of the time we want it now.

Nature teaches us patience, one of the grand lessons of the ages.

■We can know that the Creator has plans for us that far surpass anything we could design for ourselves.

Spring, with its wondrous colors and scents and scenes, far surpasses any counterfeit "natural" beauty that human beings, with all their skill, might attempt to manufacture. Nature is the ultimate artist.

Even when a stubborn winter cuts short some of spring's finest gifts, there remains more than enough to show us how grand it all is. Spring is always worth the wait.

On Using Our Storms

This column is being written during a spring storm, at home with my study windows open—open as much as the blowing rain will allow.

All the glorious sounds and aromas and sensations—even the violence—of this sudden evening turbulence are just an arm's length away, allowing an exhilarating nearness to one of nature's grand wonders and delights (accompanied, even, by an occasional splattering by wind-blown raindrops).

The evening's experience has a lesson: we too often waste our storms.

In addition to all else that spring storms do for us (who knows the mysteries of their purposes and ways?), they nourish our souls, refresh our minds, and bless our lives in immeasurable ways. Spring storms are one of life's bonuses, a banquet for our senses.

Outside my window the suddenly-cooled breeze has turned to a gusty, even chilly, wind that has set my windchimes off on a frenzied cacophony of delightful Oriental sounds. The delicate treble notes are accompanied by the thunder's booming basses, ranging from sudden clashes that seem frighteningly near to faint rumblings, sounds from some distant battlefield where the champions of justice are winning the day against the forces of evil.

The giant oak tree in my back yard, her muscles stretched and her hair shaken free by the gusting winds and slashing rain, is illuminated momentarily by flashes now silent, now followed by startling claps of thunder. Cool winds bring the aroma of wet oak and rock dust and damp moss and pine needles and lightning-charged air into my room and suddenly I'm transported to childhood, running free in the rain-fresh forests of Mount Magazine.

Storms, of course, can be dangerous. They can hurt people and destroy property. They can even cause death. Storms are to be respected, to be taken seriously.

But if spring storms are accompanied by violence, they are followed by stillness and quiet. It is as though nature, having done its spadework, will now rest awhile and let its creative processes do their silent work.

Storms remind us of a wonderful, though sometimes painful, truth: that *all* of life is a gift. And that all of it—even its storms—may be bearers of blessings, hidden though they may be.

Whopper Summers

We've been in our getting-ready-for-summer mode for about a dozen weeks now and so far nothing has happened. Summer hasn't arrived.

But we're ready. We're sittin' here waitin' for summer to hit and according to a fellow on the radio, this year's summer is going to be a whopper.

Yep, a whopper—a hot one, the radio man said. He backed up this opinion by quoting a fellow who cited chapter and verse from the *Farmer's Almanac*, that inerrant and infallible authority on such things.

If the *Farmer's Almanac* says the summer of '86 is going

to be a whopper, it's likely to be a whopper.

The radio man's comment tripped our switch, throwing us back a half-century to when we really had whopper summers, back to the time when kids were really kids, summers were really summers, and hot was really hot. Those were the real whopper summers, the summers of the early '30s, the summers long before air conditioning.

Those were the summers when your shirt stuck to the church pew on sweltering Sundays; when dogs stayed under shady bushes; when by day's end the mattress on your bed had absorbed so much heat that it never cooled, causing the sweat to roll off your neck while you tried to sleep.

Those were attic fan summers. Real whoppers.

Those were fat-duck-on-the-face summers, when the humidity was heavy as a boiled wool coat and the sun hotter than the radiator on a Model A Ford after steamin' up Mount Magazine on an August afternoon.

Those were the summers when town sidewalks and even sandy country lanes were too hot for bare feet, necessitating a hop, skip, and run to the nearest grassy spot.

We're talkin' hot, whopper summers.

Those were the summers of long droughts, when skies turned brassy and Methodists almost consented to become Baptists if it meant a dip in the town creek.

Whopper summers.

There were two best times of the day during whopper summers. One was early morning before the sun settled down to business and let you know, without a doubt, who was boss for the day.

Evening was almost as nice. Summer vacation chores for the day were over and you could rest from picking beans and sweetcorn under a sun so hot it baked your brains and air so thick you could hardly breathe and sweat so salty it stung your eyes and prickly garden things so pesky they made you itch all over.

Whopper summers.

Then came supper with fried okra and lots of iced tea with gobs of sugar and real lemon and mint and after that maybe some home-made ice cream and cake. And then perhaps games in the neighborhood, those grand twilight hide-and-seek games when the first faint currents of cool evening air found their way, mysteriously, out of the shadows of the honeysuckle and privet hedge, making even the mosquitoes almost bearable.

Come on, whopper summer! Whenever you're ready, we'll take whatever you've got and be glad in the taking.

Fireflies in a Fruit Jar

Meanwhile, if we're not careful, we'll miss one of the grand treats of the season: the coming of the fireflies.

For the perennial child in us, the first lightning bug of summer can hold an inexpressible wonder, an irrepressible primal exultation. One should watch for the first firefly of summer as for the pearl of great price.

The firefly's momentary and fleeting bit of light, its pulsating magic moving slowly in the quiet summer dusk, is capable of resurrecting an excitement and mystery that is granted to children but which, regrettably, is too often lost by adults somewhere along the way.

It is possible to be so preoccupied with things like religion and politics and morality and sin and making money and spending money that one can miss the *really* important things in life.

Like fireflies.

Fireflies invite us to wonder. They tempt us to chase them, to capture them, and, gently, to hold them captive for a time while pondering their fascinating secret. (Perhaps, even, to put them in a fruit jar overnight and—after punching holes in the lid with an ice pick—place the jar on our bedside table and drift off to sleep with its magic filling our head and saturating our memory.)

(Fireflies-in-a-fruit-jar is one of the watershed events of childhood, an epic experience for the soul.)

Fireflies tantalize us with their questions. What makes lightning bugs light? What messages are being sent by those tiny yellow turn-signals that speckle our back yards on long summer evenings? What questions—and answers—are encoded in all those blippings: to whom are they directed? Could those little golden pops of lights have some fundamental, priority role to play in the whole ultimate scheme of things? Perhaps even holding the entire universe together with their seeming insignificance?

(That's silly, of course. Isn't it? Entomologists probably could explain it all very logically in a sentence or two. But if so, I don't want to hear it. I'd rather listen to the poets ask their questions and weave their theories and be content that the queries go unanswered and that the simple beauty—and the complexity—of it all remains.)

If parables must be drawn from such ponderings, they perhaps should be kept private. All persons deserve the freedom—and the responsibility—of interpreting what their own fireflies are saying to them.

What we should be cautioned about, however, is that we not become so distracted that we miss the invitation to listen.

Of Summer Storms

One of those sudden summer storms swept through our town the other evening, and aside from a few limbs wrested from the majestic trees in the neighborhood, there was no apparent damage.

Quite the contrary, we suppose. The storm brought with it a refreshing and much-needed rainfall, giving new life to our drouth-stricken lawns and the few scraggly tomatoes and green peppers still left in our "bucket" gardens.

It isn't accurate to call such storms sudden because they do, of course, announce their approach with subtle teasings, proposals that may or may not be honored.

Such announcements come almost daily on hot summer afternoons. First come the giant, billowing thunderheads moving in from the west, prairie schooners laden with life-giving cargo. Then, with luck, may come a faint far-off rumbling that is as much felt as heard, a ruffling in the summer-heavy air that causes one to ask aloud, though others may not be present, "Is that thunder I hear?"

Again with luck, those rumblings increase to earth-shattering explosions that, one imagines, bounce along the sky for at least a couple of counties or so.

More often than not, those rumblings are accompanied by streaks and sheets of silver and purple lightning that are a wonder to behold and—so long as they behave themselves—a delight to the eye.

The whole experience is an inexpressible joy, one of those cost-nothing happenings we receive so casually, little thought given to its profound cosmic meanings and effects.

After our storm moved on the other evening, the setting sun broke through, revealing a brilliant, full-arched rainbow. Its splendid colors, bright against the dark storm clouds retreating to the east, shouted their ancient biblical benedictions of peace and hope.

Perhaps summer storms are meant to be food for our souls as well as nourishment for the earth.

In a time when human beings have so messed up the Garden with greed and racism and pride and strife, could summer storms be meant to shake up our souls, clear our heads, sharpen our vision, and renew our hope?

Perhaps so.

Then again, summer storms may not be anything more than just that—summer storms—but you'll never convince us of that, not in a million years.

Summer, Salad, and Sin

There's a rule somewhere requiring quarterly tribute to the changing of the seasons. Whenever spring comes sneaking in on the heels of winter, or summer trips lightly to the fore on some unsuspecting afternoon, or fall announces its arrival one chilly morning, words must be arranged to do proper homage to the occasion.

Religion writers are granted no immunity from the obligation.

The salad is especially nice today. Delightful. Perhaps it'll help prolong the summer. It's too soon to give up these long, delicious days with their lovely, lazy, iced tea evenings.

Too soon the cold. Too soon the snow and ice. Too soon the dark.

Fifty-three degrees! To someone outside the office, without a coat, the wind on Louisiana Street carries an unmistakable message. Low-slung clouds moving quickly from the west, white and grey against a deep-blue sky, confirm what all the senses know: fall has arrived.

That flight of ducks seen last evening is further evidence that even though the country's economy and too many other things are all messed up, nature still has its act together and knows what it's supposed to do.

It's a pity we don't learn more from the seasons. They're so dependable, so regular, so right. Although they may not always please us, we know that somehow they're doing what they're supposed to do. There's *reason* in their ways.

Such, alas, too often is more than can be said for us humans.

Christians kill Muslims, Jews kill Palestinians, Arabs kill each other; the whole Middle East seems an unbearable nightmare and our own sins are hidden awhile by the horror. Some contend the death count in the most recent massacre in Beirut may reach 1,400 or more.

"So what else is new?"

The dreaded expression, reflecting an equally fatal resignation and surrender, lurks in the mind if not on the tongue.

How long can humanity retain its capacity to be horrified at its own inhumanity? How long before terrorism and death squads and assassinations and executions and wars kill even our toughest sensitivities?

Stay, summer. Stay, fall. Stay, winter. Stay, spring. Keep us in school till our lessons are done. Show us your secrets. Give us your wisdom. Teach us the ways of God.

The bedcovers had to be pulled up the other evening, though surely there'll be Indian summer days and nights yet to enjoy. Still, it's time to get out the winter clothes, the hats, gloves, scarves, boots, and topcoats.

Perhaps, with grace, by the time summer rolls 'round once again we may have learned a thing or two more from the seasons.

Perhaps.

These little cubed beets are nice in the salad today. Fall vegetables. But summer leaves its benedictions. Come spring, the green onions will be back. And after that, the summer.

It's a promise.

Fall: Just Because

Just because this is the first day of fall doesn't mean we've got to think fall thoughts. Not at all. In fact, we're not required even to take note of the coming of the second most beautiful season of the whole year. It's not a federal offense to ignore the fall equinox on the very day it happens (at 3:33 p.m. today), even though it does occur only once a year.

Nobody can force us to think about beautiful fall days. We could, for example, think instead about politics. That would be fun. Or about religion *and* politics. That would be both fun and novel. Or about economics or the national debt or the international trade deficit or some other entertaining subject.

We don't have to glance out our window and enjoy the subtle changes taking place in the color of the trees. No police officer can make us inhale the freshness of the early morning air or take casual walks in the cool evening and enjoy a glorious sunset whose colors hint what the whole landscape will soon bring.

No one can command us to watch the sumac and sweet gum and maple and oak show off their splendid colors. Or note the days getting shorter and the nights chillier and the bedcovers feeling better and sweaters being looked forward to.

There's no law that requires us to be alert for the first whiff of fall leaves burning in someone's yard or to catch the telltale blue smoke from a neighbor's chimney, giving away the secret that yet another fall lover has been unable to put away the temptation to kindle the first offering of the season.

It's a free country. We don't have to put up with the aroma of seasoned oak crackling on an open hearth.

Nor, in this time of so much uncertainty, can anyone force us to listen to fall's message of the Creator's faithfulness. We don't have to think about the divine miracles involved in such things as planting and tilling and harvesting. We can ignore all that if we wish.

Fall is a grand teacher, a friend, a preparer for winter. But who needs friends and teachers?

Isn't it nice not to have to think about fall?

"Okay, I Take It Back"

Okay, Winter, I take it back. Most of it, that is—all those unkind things I said about you in this column a couple of months ago. That wasn't very nice. I'm sorry. Penitent, actually. The truth is, I'm really a closet lover of winter.

Closet because it's not very popular in these parts to go around saying that you like, much less love, winter. But I do. The truth is out.

Winter lovers delight in snowy days, when gentle flakes cover houses and lawns, making picture postcards of ordinary scenes. Winter lovers rejoice in bright, crisp days when sun and ice-covered trees create a sparkling, magic world. Winter lovers like it when, with fall leaves gone, the world opens up to reveal its secrets. Winter lovers like crackling wood fires and hot chocolate and toasty-warm bedcovers. Winter lovers are a special breed of people. They're the kind of folk who have that exciting, faraway look in their eyes, even indoors on dreary days. Winter lovers are the kind of people who, rather than drive to the grocery store, prefer to walk. They even like carrying the groceries home, pretending they're trudging back to their mountain cabin in the Klondike with a month's worth of life-saving supplies.

Come late fall, winter lovers get that look about them.

They're different. They glance out of windows a lot, watch the sky, always expecting snow. Winter lovers know the excitement, the joy, of anticipation.

Although winter lovers may be in the same room with you, they're not, really. They're somewhere north, or west, in the high mountains, skiing down a wintry slope or climbing a high ridge or toasting their feet before a roaring fire in their mountain hideaway.

Winter lovers begin as children whose mothers can't get them to come inside on snowy days. They start out as little boys and little girls who aren't bothered by runny noses and who lose their gloves and who always want to slide down hills just one more time.

Winter lovers are young people who as they go through the difficult adolescent years are frequently thought of as "problems." They don't mind especially well and they always have opinions of their own. They're stubborn, feisty, and—let's admit it—often difficult to live with.

Winter lovers grow up to be big boys and girls who'd rather do things their own way. It's not that they're disobedient—just independent.

And it's not that winter lovers are irresponsible. Far from it. They're probably the most dependable of all people. They're hardy. Tough. Yet, for the most part, they're gentle and loving. Winter lovers grow up to be real people.

Now, winter, am I back in your graces? I hope so.

Hmmmm. Looks like it could snow tonight.

Waiting for the Snow

One may be excused, perhaps, for mental wanderings during snow days. Or even during days when snow is forecast but hasn't arrived.

Even the thought of snow does something for the soul. There's a special grace—something fundamental, something tied to our primordial nature—about waiting for snow to fall.

The Creator must have known this. Perhaps that's the why of such days and nights. Perhaps God knew that without snow, human beings wouldn't do enough mental wandering.

It's time for another trip to the living room window, to part the curtains and peer outside to see, with the aid of the streetlight, if the snow has begun to fall.

Not yet. Back to the book, one's reading enhanced with an eager, if unrelated, anticipation.

The most casual hint that snow is expected declares recess on whatever else is going on. No matter how serious the occasion, a little snow can make the event seem insignificant, or at least worthy of postponement. How nice to have meetings—especially important ones—cancelled by the reality, or even the threat, of snow! It's particularly nice if the meetings are the kind where you have to sit a lot, listen a lot, and aren't allowed to speak very often. Snow gives such meetings a well-deserved "Cancelled!"

It looks more promising now. With care, one can detect a few scattered flakes in the streetlight's glow, little messengers of joy dancing earthward. Time to get the jogging gear on and pretend it's a burden to have to go out on a night like this.

Snow has a marvelous acoustical effect, a way of soundproofing the neighborhood. It wraps houses and yards and streets in its soft white comforter, muffling whatever noises might disrupt the peace. Yet it treats the careful listener to the gentle sounds of flakes sifting through pine needles and falling on brown oak leaves.

Running in new-fallen snow has delightful rewards. You get to hear the *crunch, crunch, crunch, crunch* of shoes on snow, and icy pellets sting your face, alerting all your senses in your late-night rendezvous with nature.

Perhaps snowy days and nights work a miracle for us by reuniting us with our childhood. Such occasions are grand "moments of grace."

Once to the Circus

All issues, questions, concerns, and activities have religious dimensions. Since creation is whole, and since flesh and spirit are inseparable, and since God created men and women in God's own image and declared all creation good, our concepts of sacred and secular are fundamentally flawed.

Question from a Friend

A friend posed the question, combining it with a statement: "I thought you were supposed to be the *religion* editor of this newspaper. What did last week's column have to do with religion?"

Ouch. Hadn't my friend ever heard of tempering the wind to the shorn lamb?

Well, let's see. Last week's column was about winter (notably a personal confession that I rather like winter). When my friend popped his question out of the blue, as they say (a religious expression), I was so flustered I couldn't come up with any defense. It didn't occur to me to respond with equal forthrightness that "only a *truly* religious person would recognize the essential religious nature of that column!" (Why don't I think of such responses when I need them?)

Nor did it occur to me to tell my friend that since God created winter, and since confession (which is what I was engaging in—being penitent over earlier unkind comments about winter) is a religious exercise, such comments should easily qualify as "religious" writing.

And besides, since winter is cold and hell is supposed to be hot, shouldn't winter be an especially religious topic? And since writing about winter requires an elevated state of mind, even of soul, and since heaven is elevated, doesn't it follow that writing about such things is a distinctly religious activity?

And so on.

But, of course, the question concerning what is and what isn't religious is an old, honored one and merits a more serious response.

Philosophers and theologians through the ages, strolling on lonely beaches and closeted in solemn contemplation, have pondered the question. Preachers have preached it. College sophomores have debated it. Religious zealots have argued it, even fought over it.

With all that in mind, we herewith offer to solve the ancient mystery: there *aren't* any "unreligious" topics! All issues, questions, concerns, and activities have religious dimensions. Since creation is whole, and since flesh and spirit are inseparable, and since God created men and women in God's own image and declared all creation good, our concepts of sacred and secular are fundamentally flawed.

It is a misunderstanding of the essential unity of life—its "religious" nature—to divide life into sacred and secular, religious and nonreligious, compartments.

There are, certainly, "irreligious" ways to talk and write about most anything. But, I say to my friend, it is not possible to find a totally non-religious topic.

Now—how 'bout them Hogs!

"Are You a Christian?"

Two recent happenings introduced issues that are difficult to deal with in print. But they are important issues that are, one suspects, of concern to many people.

The happenings were a telephone call and a letter.

On the long-distance call I was talking with a very pleasant man, whom I had never met, who was giving information about a church event.

After the caller had given the relevant data he paused and said, "There's one more thing. May I ask you a question?"

Certainly, I said.

"Are you a Christian?"

It would seem that after almost 57 years one would have learned how to field that question. But I confess that I never have. And, in a society that expects rock-ribbed certainty from those who profess religious faith, that's not a comfortable confession to make.

With all due respect to the caller, whose sincerity and good intentions I do not question, I suggest there's something wrong with the question in the context in which it was asked.

There are, of course, many Christians who see the question as legitimate—even mandatory—in any circumstance. While appreciating religious fervor and conviction, I submit there's another point of view.

First off, the question, in my understanding, is not the kind that two previously unintroduced persons can entertain with spiritual and intellectual integrity while the long-distance telephone meter is running. It's the kind of question that invites other than single-syllable or even several paragraph answers. Religious witness dismissed, simply by answering a question.

The question introduces issues and invites debate on numerous other questions, themselves very important. Those questions have to do with the nature of religious witness and what "being a Christian" is all about.

"Being Christian," I submit, is not so much a matter of what one is as what one is *becoming*. It is not being able to offer a simple, unagonized "Yes" to what is an ultimate question.

Why such concern over the question? It seems an irreverent impertinence to claim for oneself what only God can affirm.

There is, indeed, a very public aspect to legitimate biblical faith and witness. But there also is a very private dimension to such things. The proper arenas are not always easily defined, but the distinction must always be acknowledged.

Furthermore, the casual question "Are you a Christian?" fails to acknowledge, much less offer acceptance of, the role of doubt—a very legitimate element in the authentic search for religious faith. Beware the person who professes to have no doubts about religion. Alfred,

Lord Tennyson, said it: "There lives more faith in honest doubt, believe me, than in half the creeds."

What is the need for faith—a "leap"—if there is no doubt? What is the need for belief if everything is "known fact"?

Much in the Bible suggests that the seeker, even the doubter, is more welcome by God than is the bellicose believer whose faith is unexamined.

If the unexamined life is not worth living, the unquestioned faith is not worth professing.

The second event noted above was a sensitive, poignant letter from a public school teacher who asked how, in keeping with the concept of separation of church and state, Christian teachers may give proper witness to their religious faith while on the job.

There's a relationship between the telephone question and the letter.

Elie Wiesel, the noted author and Holocaust survivor, said in a recent lecture in Little Rock that he believes that by being a good Jew he is helping Christians be good Christians and other person be better adherents to whatever religious faith they profess.

Could it be that Christian evangelism has more to do with *service* to one's fellow human beings than with efforts to convert them? Could it be that authentic religious witness has more to do with respect for another's religious persuasion than in pointing to one's own faith?

About My Friends

I've got this friend, see, who's consistently harassed because she's a liberal. I've got this other friend who's continually maligned because he's a conservative. I like my friends and it's no fun seeing them pushed around.

So here's a word for the harassers and maligners: don't mess with my friends.

All of which is to say we've got a problem—or that we've *still* got a problem: a shortage of tolerance for other people's religious convictions. So what else is new.

I've got some other friends. Among them are Jews who are the constant object of conversion attempts by Christians. And there are my Catholic friends, who some Protestants believe hide guns in their basements, silently waiting to take over the United States government and the Republic of Whatever.

And don't forget my Muslim friends who are suspected by some perfectly good Christians and others of being racists and worse.

And don't forget my "Moonie" friends, who somehow are able to evoke the most un-Christian attitudes and responses from otherwise good Christian people.

And then there are my Unitarian friends, who some folks say have no religion at all. These religionists are bold enough to suggest that matters of faith are just that—matters of faith, not subject to nor requiring "proof." These friends say that to require proof of matters of faith is to insult those matters. These friends also are bold enough to suggest, with the poet Alfred, Lord Tennyson, that "there lives more faith in honest doubt than in half the creeds."

What is one to do with one's friends?

Then there are those friends who insist on the inerrancy and infallibility of the Bible. Some folks say they're rednecks. There are, too, those friends who say that to insist on the literal inerrancy of the Bible is to make an idol—a god—of that which the Creator didn't intend to be an idol. Some of these friends are bold enough to suggest that faith is more a matter of the heart than the head.

Some of my friends insist that to be tolerant of all religions is to believe in none, that acceptance of all religions reflects an absence of conviction about any religion.

I can talk some straightforward theological language with these friends: phooey.

I suggest, rather, that an attitude of openness to others' religious convictions reflects not only good manners (not a bad religious attribute, by the way) but a compassionate spirit, a praiseworthy benevolence, and a mature spirituality that is more at home with Jesus and the prophets of the world's other religions than is a strident, radical, close-minded exclusiveness.

So there.

A Midsummer Dream

I had this dream the other night and haven't gotten over it yet.

In the dream I beheld a large banquet table at which were seated representatives from all the world's religions. (I didn't see who got to say grace.)

Christians were seated beside Hindus, Jews by Muslims, Animists by Buddhists, Zoroastrians across the table from Shintoists, and so on. Even the atheists were there.

It was quite a sight. Catholics and Protestants from Northern Ireland were friendly with each other. Muslim sectarians were having peaceful conversations together. Israelis and Palestinians were praying together and Bahais and Muslims from Iran were smiling at one another, laughing together. There were even—wonder of wonders—some Southern Baptist "fundamentalists" chatting amicably with a bunch of the denomination's "moderates." A couple of well-known religious righters had their arms around the president of the National Council of Churches and the chaplain of the National Organization of Women, all having a great time.

And there were a couple of big-time television preachers laughing and carrying on with some folks from the American Civil Liberties Union and Handgun Control, Inc.

And I caught a glimpse of some United Methodists actually talking with a leader of the Unification Church, a "Moonie." I even saw some Presbyterian main-liners chatting with some of those other kinds of Presbyterians.

And I thought I saw, though I may be mistaken, an Episcopalian drinking strawberry soda pop with a Pentecostal!

It was, as I said, quite a dream.

When, on the next evening, the dream recurred, I thought I ought to check things out with a couple of my most trusted advisers, my pastor and my doctor.

My reverend paused a moment, seemingly pondering the possibility for some profound, prophetic pronouncement. He spoke:

"Sounds goofy to me," he said.

My doctor, after checking several doctor books, said he had it figured out. "Bad potato salad," he said, reaching for his prescription pad.

Seeing I was still in need, my two counselors put their heads together and came up with some advice.

"Take a couple of days off, friend. You've been work-ing too hard. This summer heat can do strange things to your head.

"And if the dream recurs, remember it was just that—a dream."

A Tale Almost Recalled

If I don't forget all this before my fingers stop typing, I suppose I ought to confess.

Some months ago my wife and I moved to Conway to be with my mother, who at 85 years confesses that her memory never was as good as it used to be.

The other day, while doing all those things necessary in getting ready to sell her twelve-year-old car, we began a search for the vehicle title.

And we searched.

Finally, after sifting through a ton of old insurance papers, outdated bills, and auto registration cards, we decided the sought-for document must be down at the bank, in the lock box.

I have just come from walking, here in the Gazette building, the near half-city-block distance between my cubicle and the microwave oven where I cook my just-mixed instant coffee. On this trip, however, when I got back to my cubicle I couldn't find my coffee cup.

Of course I couldn't. It was still in the cooker thing. I had carried a letter along with me on the hike, had gotten engrossed in reading it, and had returned sans coffee cup.

An understandable lapse.

Now—back to the engrossing tale of the search for the lost title. The reason we were searching for the title is that we were going to buy a new car, see, which my mother and my wife would share.

So, in an effort to wean my mother away from driving her old car, a full-sized larger type, I suggested that on our trip to the bank to search for the title she drive my wife's car, one of those smaller models akin to the new one we were to buy. This necessitated a driving lesson, which I proceeded to give before we left the carport.

Once under way, things went well. For two whole

blocks. Then we came to the stop sign at the intersection of Davis and Caldwell Streets. Decision time. My little mother, full of pride that we had come so far so safely, looked over at me and asked: "Now where is it we're going?"

It's good that Mother and I have my wife, what's-her-name, to look after us.

Now, for those of you who insist on having "something religious" in this corner, we offer the following brief homily.

One of the indispensable functions of the church and synagogue is that they serve as society's "rememberers." They help a world that is short on memory. The biblical religions remind us not only of who we are and Whose we are, but of where we're going and what we are meant to do along the way.

Next time you see a church steeple, try to remember those things it would do all of us well to recall.

Tough Assignment

Sensitive religious people (can there really be any other authentic kind?) have a tough assignment in this age of confrontation: to be faithful to their conviction—and to do so in a manner that doesn't violate the rights of others and that is consistent with the religious principles they seek to uphold—and at the same time to be reconcilers in the midst of discord, fulfilling the ministry of reconciliation.

It's a tough assignment indeed. How can one be a true, vigorous advocate of his or her particular religious beliefs and yet be understanding toward other positions, and loving toward their adherents, and at the same time be a reconciling presence amidst the alienation that inevitably accompanies differences of religious conviction?

Consider the current challenge, some of the many volatile issues that evoke strong feelings, foster hostile attitudes and actions, and frequently set otherwise amicable people against each other. The list is long: abortion, creation science and evolution, different views of Bible interpretation, capital punishment, arms control and defense, registration for a possible military draft, minority rights, women's issues, and others. Is it any wonder ours is called an age of confrontation?

We suggest the following as hints toward discovering answers to the dilemma:

■First, the asking of a fundamental question and the probing required to find the answers: What, really, is the *purpose* of religion and of religious faith? Why religious faith anyway?

Is "true," authentic religion a set of doctrines to be defended—or is it a way of life to be lived? Is it a rigid "faith position" to be vigorously propagated—or is it a spirit of love and service and justice and mercy to be expressed in attitudes and deeds? Is it a particular way or method or "school" of interpreting the Bible—or is it an effort to discover the larger spirit and message of the Book and its Author, a celebration of the mighty acts and victories of God, an effort to be more "truly human" beings?

■Second, we suggest that the dilemma is put into perspective by some guidelines for relationships with persons whose religious beliefs differ from one's own:

Do I give the other person and his or her convictions the same respect I want for myself and my own beliefs? Am I willing to enter into true discussion—genuine dialogue—and not just a monologue in which one party is eager to talk but unwilling to listen? Do I refrain from judgments that are not mine to make? Do I maintain the kind of humility consistent with the highest biblical spirit—am I willing to admit I may be wrong? And am I willing to acknowledge that to "win" an argument about religion may well be to lose it?

Few dimensions of religious life attract so much attention these days as do the differences that divide various religious groups. Those groups would do well to realize that the secular world is looking on at such times, taking note of the example being set.

The situation suggests a priority question: What's happening to us as we debate our differences about religion? Do we like what we see? If not, can we do anything about it?

Thoughts While Mowing

It occurred to me while mowing the lawn the other evening that this is the ninth year I've done this chore (where we presently live) and each year I've followed the same mowing pattern, precisely.

You may want to take notes on this:

First I mow the back yard (always in two segments, moving counter-clockwise), then the back side-yard (mowing between the shrubs first and then along the street), then the east side-yard (moving the large rocks along the driveway, mowing between them, and then replacing them), then attacking the largest segment, the front yard (following a time-proven and somewhat complex pattern that, unfortunately, I don't have the space or patience to describe for you), and then, between circles around the front yard, working in the west side-yard (a pushover).

Then comes the process of blowing the grass off the sidewalks, with the mower on high speed. Following that comes the ritual of putting the mower away in the metal shed that our youngest son and I assembled Saturday, September 8, 1979 (it says so in a scratched-in note on the inside wall).

Following that, the door is locked and, in a final and important part of the ritual, the first two numbers of the combination lock are dialed so there will be just two numbers remaining to be selected when, in my haste, I'm eager to mow again the next Friday evening or Saturday morning.

(You're probably fascinated by all this and yearning for more details, but this will have to suffice.)

Now—there's something either very right or very unnecessary about all this devotion to routine. Either the first time I mowed the lawn, nine years ago, I did it the only absolutely correct way and there's no possibility of improving on my sure-fire technique—or else I'm so set in my ways that I'm not about to change, even in the manner in which I go about mowing my lawn.

I think I know which it is.

But whatever, all this suggests an always timely topic: to what extent are we so wedded to our ways that we close ourselves off to new possibilities, new discoveries, new ways of thinking, new ways of doing things?

It's a question that is especially appropriate regarding religion. For, like it or not, religious people have a reputation of being among the most firmly set-in-their-ways people on earth (and, perhaps, in heaven, too). That can be both good and bad. One of the great contributions of religious faith is that it speaks of those great realities and grand truths that remain constant when other things are changing.

But there's another side of this coin. The biblical narrative also reveals a God who makes Himself known through change. He is a God who, by a pillar of fire by night and a cloud by day, leads His people from the safe familiarities of a known land to the insecurities of an unknown one. He invites them to search, through myriads of changes, for a city that is not easily found.

So, here's something to think about the next time you mow your lawn: are there elements of my religious life, its beliefs and practices, that need changing? Am I willing to accept the risks that such changes may entail? Those are tough questions.

And who knows? There might even be a better master plan for mowing my lawn. But I doubt it.

What It Was Was Religion

We had never met, the gentleman across the dining table at a public gathering this week and I. After introducing ourselves we made conversation while waiting for the program to begin.

"Oh, yes—you write for the *Gazette*, don't you. I've seen your columns. They're on the church page, aren't they. As I recall, not all of them are about religion. Are they?"

Caught off guard, I wasn't sure how to respond to the comment, which came across as a totally charitable one. I think I mumbled something about believing that *all* subjects are about religion—or, at least, that religion has something to do with all subjects.

Just as I had regrouped and put together a dandy, sure-fire defense, the presiding officer asked everyone to stand and sing "God Bless America." I learned long ago that there are two songs—"The Star-Spangled Banner" is the other—that are hard to sing while trying to make your point in a theological debate. So I sang that God would bless America and prayed that he would bless me and waited to resume the dialogue.

As we sat down, I learned forward to reopen my case. But a visiting bishop, the principal speaker, was being introduced and since I was sitting right smack in front of

44

him I figured it wouldn't be proper to use the occasion to impress my new friend with my seventeen reasons why *all* subjects are, in fact, religious and therefore fair game for religion writers. So, with no little consternation, I let the whole thing pass.

The brief encounter brought to mind an important dimension of the ongoing national debate about the role of religious faith in a secular society: whether religion has to do only with certain aspects of life—"religious" subjects—or whether it has to do with *all* of life.

I would have suggested to my new friend that the biblical religions opt for the latter contention—that religion is a way of life that encompasses the whole, that relates to all that human beings do, think, are, and are capable of doing and thinking and becoming.

It would be easier if religion could be relegated to one corner of our lives. Things would be more comfortable if we didn't have to measure our deeds with the yardstick of religious morality and ethics.

It would be easier if we could hold our opinions and make our laws about such things as nuclear weapons and foreign policy and capital punishment and alcohol and the sick and the poor without being bothered with such concepts as love, justice, mercy, and—God forbid—divine judgment.

It would be easier if we could fill out our income tax forms and buy and sell our goods and services and not have to worry about something called honesty.

What are those issues that are not in some way related to religion or religion to them? None comes to mind.

Such an understanding makes for a lot of abuses and misuses of religion, to be sure. But the alternative is worse.

Perhaps many of the problems upon us these days have come because we choose to believe that certain areas of our lives are off-limits to God and to the implications of religious faith. A country that tries to make it on that kind of philosophy won't have to be bothered long with singing such songs as "God Bless America."

Things to Sneeze At

Sneezing, admittedly, is not your most religious of subjects. But neither is it the most irreligious. So, in this post-Lenten season when all the really religious topics have already been written about, sneezing will have to do. It is not, one might say, a topic to be sneezed at.

The subject comes to mind because we're in the sneezing season, when nature puts all those little things in the air that cause us to sneeze. Many of us know about such things. We sneeze a lot during this time of the year. I do. My wife does. A lot of my friends and acquaintances do. Sneezing, one could say, is in the air these days.

It's not particularly fun, all this sneezing. It's serious business. Not to be sneezed at.

Take the expression itself—"not to be sneezed at." Although we wouldn't pretend to be the final authority on such things, the expression would appear to mean that a matter is not to be taken lightly, that it is worthy of more than just being brushed aside (blown aside?) with a sneeze.

Such an analysis, we submit, is not to be sneezed at.

This whole "sneezed at" business should not be spared the benefits of theological examination. If there are things that are not to be sneezed at, it follows that there are things that *ought* to be sneezed at.

What, one could ask, are those things in religion that deserve being sneezed at?

Only a fool would attempt to answer that question.

The following is an attempt to answer that question. And none of these answers is to be sneezed at:

■Religion that puts more emphasis on outward appearance than inward reality merits a great big sneeze.

■Religion that puts self before others, that emphasizes gratification of personal material desires, should be sneezed at.

■Religion that deepens without widening and widens without deepening deserves a big "ka-CHOO!"

■Religion that spends all of its time in the sanctuary and none in the streets is sneezable religion.

■Religion that spends all of its time in the streets and none in the sanctuary deserves the hanky.

■Religion that haggles over the Scripture's every jot and tittle but trips lightly over the difficult demands wins the Big Sneeze award.

■And religion that is satisfied only by listing all those things that are wrong with other people's religion ought to be sneezed at good and proper.

It's No Wonder

Religious folks are becoming a bit testy these days and it's no wonder.

What with the antics of a few highly visible television evangelists commanding the spotlight, a lot of religious groups are catching it on the chin.

The bad deeds of the few are reflecting on the many. Legitimate religion is being tarred with the same brush applied to the Elmer Gantrys.

It is not a happy time in the sanctuary.

But hold on. Let's look at all this.

We heard a United Methodist bishop say it this week: we should never be surprised at sin.

How true. The church, of all institutions, ought not to be surprised by sin. Current wrong-doings, among church leaders and others, confirm what the church has been preaching for centuries: people *are* (pardon the word) sinners. Yep—even you nice folks who read these words and the one who writes them. Sinners, all.

That fact, of course, doesn't excuse religious leaders

from doing their best to overcome the condition. If gold rusts, what will iron do, as the saying goes.

Here goes with some unsolicited, free counsel to religious leaders for such a time:

■Welcome the exposure of charlatans and hypocrites. Be glad, though remorseful, when wrong-doing is revealed.

■Don't kill the messenger. While sleaze journalism is itself to be exposed and condemned, don't blame the media for reporting what's happening. The church, of all institutions, should be the most enthusiastic "freedom of information" advocate.

■Examine your own house. Clean up your own laundry. Demand integrity from others only after you demand it of yourself.

■Do your job as never before. Keep on with the task at hand. Feed the hungry. Comfort the sorrowing. Preach good news and proclaim hope throughout the land. And don't pull your prophetic punches. There are still a bunch of scoundrels out there who need to hear the thunder of righteousness and the call for justice to roll down like water. Sic 'em.

■Above all else, remember who you are—proponents of truth, forgiveness, redemption, reconciliation, and love.

■Finally, don't worry abut the future of the church—or about your own perception by a secular society. We suspect the public is smart enough to know the value of true and honest religion.

Keep your eyes on the Lord and do your work as best you can.

That's it. Sermon's over. Amen.

(You don't have to send money.)

Once to the Circus

Having been to the circus with my grandchildren this week, I'm reminded of a story. It seems that a youngster, a resident of a small town, had never seen a circus. One day the report came that the Greatest Show on Earth, en route to a large city, would stop in the small town for a one-evening performance.

There was a problem, though. The performance was to be on a Sunday. The youngster, knowing his mother's insistence that he be in prayer meeting every Wednesday night and at church each Sunday morning and evening, knew his chances of seeing the circus were slim indeed.

After delivering herself of a lecture on the proper observance of Sunday and the virtues of holy living, the mother finally gave in to the youngster's pleadings. He would be allowed, this one time, to go to the circus on Sunday.

After the big show was over and the young boy returned home, his mother asked what he thought of the show.

With visions of daring young men on the flying trapeze, elephants, and clowns still in his head, the young boy replied, "Mama, if you ever get to go to the circus, just once, you'll never want to go to church again!"

Most veteran churchgoers—at least those who've been to a circus—know the feeling.

We once heard the same conclusion expressed another way, this time by someone who knows better, the veteran wife of a veteran preacher. This good woman had faithfully accompanied her Methodist "presiding elder" husband on what must have seemed an interminable summer-long schedule of revival meetings.

After a particularly exhausting week of "protracted

meetings," as such revivals were accurately identified in those days, the minister's long-suffering wife exclaimed, "Oh, mercy, I'm *so* tired." And then, as if a vision had appeared, she added with a sigh, "But maybe there'll be no church in heaven!"

If there has to be some justification for telling such stories, in defense of the church, perhaps it's that nobody ever promised churchgoers a circus every week. Or an easy time of it.

But in fact, the circus analogy is not altogether out of place with regard to the church. True worship is a grand celebration, properly accompanied by excitement and prospects of abiding joy.

Although church-going is serious business, not designed to provide laughs and entertainment, the thought is worthy of pondering; true religion is not unlike the circus. It offers mystery, miracle, risk, and a glow that lingers through the years.

Once one has truly worshipped, all of life—even, or perhaps especially, the circus!—takes on added meaning.

Along the Way

The biblical religions remind us not only of who we are and Whose we are, but of where we're going and what we're meant to do along the way.

Sometimes the Sea

Sometimes it's the mountains, sometimes the sea. Or perhaps the desert. Or the high plains. But whatever, there are places where the mind likes to travel and the body is unable to go.

It's an ancient, inborn restlessness. A form of searching, or seeking. Some would call it a disaffection with one's situation but I submit that it is, rather, a wanderlust of divine origin, a yearning that the Creator has placed, with intention, into the hearts of all human beings. We are created to be seekers—strangers and sojourners on a divine trail, hounds of earth sired by the Hound of Heaven, hot on the scent of Truth. It is, in a totally inadequate expression, the name of the game. How poor we would be without it.

The question at hand is what one does with such a drive. A hint at one response comes from an author, his name now unrecalled, who entitled his autobiography *Issues That Have Used My Life*.

That's it, precisely. What are those issues—those causes, values, and interests—that we allow to "use" our lives? To what purpose do we spend our years? What searches do we consider worthy of a life investment? What battles are really worth the fighting?

One's own life-search is one's own business, of course. But it is significant that humanity has been most enriched by those who have invested their lives in the more noble causes. Our literature praises the teachers, the healers, the peacemakers, the reconcilers, the reformers, the crusaders for justice and righteousness.

"Let us now praise famous men," an ancient liturgy invokes. "Those who ruled in their kingdoms and were renowned by their power ..., leaders of the people in their deliberations ..., wise in their instructions .... All these were honored in their generation and were a glory in their times."

It is an understatement to say there are numerous noble causes these days in desperate need of advocates. Not so frequently noted is the good news that there is a growing number of persons willing to join up and be counted. Whether it's to provide their own communities with better schools or to crusade for a peaceful planet, there is a swelling tide of concern over important issues of the day.

Such a reality is more than wishful thinking. It's a phenomenon worthy of celebration. With all the bad news around these days, the Creator must be delighted to see the hounds of earth hot on the trail, yelping at the heels of humanity's largest enemies, pursuing its grandest visions.

Yelp on, oh daughters and sons of God!

The Ultimate Questions

They are, of course, the ultimate questions, at least for persons confronting them at the moment: How does one deal with a terminal illness? How do we prepare for the death of a family member or friend? What does one say to a loved one who is dying? How do we best relate to friends who are experiencing such sorrows and trials?

Those are the priority questions alongside which all other questions, no matter how urgent, pale in comparison. Sooner or later the questions come to us all. And when they do, they rearrange our lives. They determine our agendas. They confront us with emotions and thoughts we otherwise resist.

Perhaps the first reaction when such questions are posed is to hasten to answer them, or attempt to answer them—to make words in an effort to be helpful. But on reflection, it occurs that perhaps the greater service is to be less concerned with "answers" and more concerned with something that might be called "the quality of presence."

This is not to say there are no helpful, practical verbal responses that can be learned regarding such crises. There are, of course, and gratefully so. It is no disparagement of those responses, however, to say there is something more important. That something, we again submit, is "presence."

The concept of presence is a frequent theme in the biblical narrative—as, for example, when the divine Presence attended Israel in its greatest times of need. The theme is reiterated in the concepts of "covenant," "congregation," "communion," "fellowship," and "the people of God." In biblical tradition, "presence" is both a divine and human ministry, one of the worshipping and serving community of faith.

For Christians, the ultimate expression of presence is the Incarnation—that God, the supreme Creator and Lord and Judge and Redeemer, was "in" Christ, reconciling the world unto Himself. He is the great Comforter, Sustainer, and Friend. In Christianity, the Incarnation is the ultimate expression of what is intended to be a common duty among people of faith: the ministry of presence.

When such theological jargoning is done with, a beautiful and simple and yet profound truth remains: "being there" is the finest, truest help one can give to loved ones and friends in moments of crisis. Such presence makes up for our stumbling efforts to "say the right thing." Such presence is, in itself, an eloquence that mere words can never equal.

Such presence doesn't attempt to deny or explain away the pain of sorrow. It acknowledges and seeks to enter into those experiences, to share them with the hope of relieving, if even a bit, their burden.

In times of need, words are important and can be helpful. But even more so is the biblical quality of "presence."

Time-Pondering Season

We'll never know who said it first: "My, how time does fly!" Not that it makes a lot of difference who said it first. It's an astute, elemental observation.

But it does make a lot of difference that time flies. For indeed it does. Time goes by. Time is an elusive, ever-moving gift, a golden butterfly forever evading its would-be captors. Time flies.

Not everyone, however, perceives time as flying. For many people, time is not a butterfly; it's a turtle. It does everything but fly. It drags. It's heavy in its tracks. It stands still.

But however time is perceived, it remains that it passes. An old book puts it this way: three things do not return—the spoken word, the spent arrow, and time passed.

Surely time ranks with love, spring, motherhood, and roses as having had wise, philosophical things said in its honor. Time, one might say, is an ever-flowing stream. Or the river one goes a-fishing in. Or a peddler who deals in dust. Or an old man waiting for the birth of his great-grandchildren. Or a benefactor. Or a friend. Or—less benevolently—a thief or a cad or an enemy. And so on and on and on until the everlasting end thereof.

Time is a squanderer of words, the victor over those who would name it and thus render it impotent. Time is Johnson grass.

Mid-August is as good a season as any—perhaps better than most—to ponder the mysteries of time. Long, hot dog-days, with crackly dry evenings when the air is filled with haze and the first hints of autumn begin to appear, are tailor-made for time-pondering.

The world's great religions have had more to say about time than have any other sources of wisdom. Generally, they view time as the mysterious yet glorious gift of God, friend to the Creator's purposes, ever serving the Divine plan.

The biblical faiths regard human beings as nothing less than stewards of such a grand prize, co-creators with God, keepers of the Creator's mysteries. To be stewards of time! It's an exciting, totally humbling thought. In one of their grander gifts, the biblical religions admonish us to become friends, rather than adversaries, of time.

One of the best assurances of immortality is that we invest our lives in those things that endure, that will outlive us. Time invites us to do that. Among such things are peace and love and reconciliation and harmony and friendship and goodwill and good works.

Such doings should keep us busy till spring arrives. Then, with spirits lifted afresh, we can continue the task.

In Search of John Wayne

It's been said that we live in an age that is without its heroes—or at least without the type of heroes that received such widespread adoration a generation or so ago. "They don't make that kind any more" is the frequently heard comment. Where have all the John Waynes gone?

One is more likely these days to hear of the antihero, counter-culture figures who seek the violent overthrow of society. But whatever, the subject prompts some questions: Is it really true that the age of heroes has passed? Are we truly without classic hero types today? And if so, is that necessarily bad? Could it be that the absence of concern over such heroes is a sign that society is maturing? These questions merit attention because they force us to examine our values and define our terminology, two things we don't especially enjoy doing.

It could be argued that the yearning for heroes reflects a weakness in society, a need to identify in others what we fail to find in ourselves. To have such heroes, the argument goes, is a cop-out, a fundamental evasion of responsibility.

There's another problem with the classic concept of hero: it's basically a sexist idea, prejudicial to women. It perpetuates a negative, even destructive, macho mentality. It frequently has been the progenitor of militarism, the breeder of violence, the father of wars. Such a concept smothers that true humanity—that humaneness, compassion, and essential gentleness—that is the soul of authentic heroism. This popular concept of a hero fails to acknowledge that true heroism is a human quality, not simply a bravadoism peculiar to rough-and-tough males.

We submit that there are heroes to be found today, and in more places than one might imagine. Consider their qualities:

■Those who continue to keep faith even though confronted with disappointment, tragedy, illness, pain, prolonged suffering, the death of loved ones, and other sorrows and hardships. Those who persevere through the dark night of the soul are heroes.

■Those who, against the odds, refuse to give way to despair. Those who, in the face of all evidence to the contrary, keep faith in their fellow human beings, hold onto their belief in God, and maintain confidence in their own potential to make a difference in the world.

■Those who, though confronted with hate, continue to love.

■Those who do battle for noble causes, who see through the shallow values of a secular, materialistic society and have dedicated their lives to a more excellent way.

■Those whose love of country reflects an equal love for all people in all countries, whose patriotism is measured by a grander scale than narrow nationalism.

■Those who, though they have fallen, pick themselves up again, take up their task, and "keep on keeping on."

Such people keep life going for all around them. They are owed more than can be imagined. They are our day's authentic heroes.

A Mid-Freeway Crisis

While driving to work the other morning in my eighteen-year-old Volkswagen "beetle," and brooding over the fact that it won't be long before my age equals the legal speed limit, I heard a fellow on the radio say that never again will a bald-headed man be elected president.

I didn't need that. I was having enough trouble settling down after being almost run off the freeway by a gentleman in a brand-new silver Cadillac Diesel who, it occurs on reflection, was disgustingly young and had hair all over his head.

The fellow also had a deep tan (gained, I surmised, from a week on the slopes at Snowmass) that looked great with his white shirt and pin-striped suit. His whole presence was appropriately accentuated by a striking young blonde woman (with matching tan) seated by his side. I supposed they were hurrying to the stockholders' meeting.

The radio man was trying to make the point that in our success-oriented and youth-worshipping society we judge people more by the package than its content. Hence, with all the emphasis on outward appearance, bald-headed men are among society's most maligned and victimized creatures.

"Amen," I muttered as my VW backfired and slipped out of gear. I had always believed that. "Preach on, brother," I mumbled to the radio.

But then it occurred to me that if I *really* believe that we judge people too much by outward appearances, I had wronged the Cadillac couple. I repented. I decided they were a seminary student and a social worker on their way to the rescue mission to speak against Mr. Reagan's welfare budget cuts.

By this time I was in the vicinity of Immanuel Baptist Church and was moved to think religious thoughts. Like, for example, that the Bible has quite a bit to say about such things as judging people only on appearances.

It's not a new problem and it has some pretty pesky current expressions. Consider a few:

■The way Christians sometimes regard each other. Liberal Christians often judge conservative Christians—and vice versa—without really trying to get to know them as individuals or to understand their story or learn why they believe and feel the way they do.

■The way Americans tend to think that all "revolutionaries" are Communists—without taking into consideration any history of social oppression, economic injustice, human rights violations, or a host of other factors that might be relevant.

■The way majorities view minorities—and vice versa—and fail to examine the *reasons* for their particular biases.

By the time I coasted into the parking lot I was convinced that most of this world's problems could be laid at the feet of all those people who judge only on appearances.

It's nice not to be afflicted with such prejudice. I have always refused to think of myself as being bald. I can't help it if all those other folks are hairy.

In Search of Wisdom

On reflection, it is difficult to find any of the characters in the Bethlehem manger scene who are not tremendously interesting, who do not pique our curiosity. Whether it's the angels or the shepherds or the wise men, all are grand subjects for pondering. But in this day when authentic wisdom is such a sought-after quality and when genuinely wise persons seem such a rarity, our vote for the Most Valuable Player award goes to the wise men.

Wise men. There's a grandness, a great comfort in the characterization. Wise persons carry a special grace with them. They are a "presence." Wise persons are a valued, indispensable gift to society. How reassuring it is to have such people around.

But like prophets, wise men and women also can be a bother. They can be a nuisance and an embarrassment—even a threat. It must have been said of a wise person: "What this world needs most is fewer people telling us what this world needs most."

Wisdom, as with truth, has a cutting edge as well as a healing one. As the prophet's role sometimes is to afflict the comfortable, as well as comfort the afflicted, wise persons bear insight and counsel that frequently are as upsetting as they are reassuring. As of old, their counsel is a mixture of good news and bad news.

The trouble with wise persons is that they always seem to be right—a circumstance that is a particular irritation if their rightness happens to expose our wrongness.

Consider the ways of the wise:

■Wise persons listen more than they speak.

■Wise persons are not so much concerned with "answers" as they are with right questions.

■Wise persons live more by the compass than the speedometer.

■Wise persons shun expediency in favor of long-haul "rightness." They are concerned with values, such as morality and justice and truth. They know the perils of covetousness and greed. They know the dangers of pride.

■Wise persons are open to new ideas and new solutions to old problems. They refuse to be captives to tradition for tradition's sake. They are willing to venture, to risk, to dare.

■Wise persons have learned the secret of mixing common sense and well-honed intellect. As witness the wise men at the manger, they know the vital role of the spirit. They know the indispensable role of the Divine. Wise persons know when to follow a star.

One could do worse than reflect on the wise men of Bethlehem and ponder awhile on what true wisdom means for such a time as ours.

"Write About Spring"

I have this friend, see, who writes a newspaper column and he frequently complains—quite frequently complains—that he can't think of anything to write about. He acts like he expects sympathy.

But I know better. Sympathy is the one thing you never offer a newspaper writer. Tough love perhaps, but not sympathy. Giving sympathy to writers is like saying "amen" to preachers. It only encourages them.

So, what to do to help my friend?

"Write about spring," I told him one rainy Monday morning.

"Humph," he said. "It's the middle of summer."

I told him that didn't make any difference, that I'd done it a hundred times.

"I know," he grimaced.

I told my friend he reminded me of a little boy I once knew. About midway through every three-months-long summer vacation this little chap would begin bugging his mother with the interminable question, "What can I do now, Mommy?"

"What did she tell him?" my friend asked.

I don't know, I said. The little boy didn't tell me.

All of which brings us to that other interminable question, the one with ultimate dimensions and the one, we suggest, that all of us would do well to entertain these days: what, indeed, *can* we do now?

The question invites some preachin':

We can make peace, not war.

We can strive to do right.

We can be good stewards of the planet.

We can take the Lord's admonition—that really tough one—and love our enemies.

We can judge not, lest we be judged.

I suggested all this to my friend. "It's as simple as that," I said.

His response, I thought, was a bit irreverent: "And we can quit giving advice to other people."

Humph, indeed.

But my friend agreed. He'd be willing to try some of those things. "At least it's better than writing about spring," he mumbled.

It was an uncalled-for comment and it provoked a parting shot: "And when you're through with all those things," I yelled, "come on back. There's more."

He hasn't been back. I guess he's still working at it.

A Tiny, Slender Thread

It occurred to us the other day that we all hang by a slender thread of grace.

That's right. We all hang by a tiny, slender thread of grace.

If that sounds too theological, forgive us. We can't think of any other word that expresses what we're trying to say.

About the best and briefest definition of grace we've run across is that it's "the unmerited favor of God." Grace is God's love for us freely given, not dependent on any merit of our own—and not counting our demerits.

This theology attack struck us the other day as we contemplated the stress being experienced within so many religious groups these days. First there are the Southern Baptists, weary with their eight-year controversy that has threatened to split the country's largest Protestant body and has weakened its evangelism and mission programs and tried its spirit.

Then there are this country's Catholics, sore beset with mounting tensions between the church in the United States and the Vatican. And as if that weren't enough, American Catholics have been squabbling amongst themselves like a bunch of Baptists—over such things as the role of women in the church, whether priests ought to be allowed to marry, family planning, and ministry to homosexuals.

And time would fail us to tell of the Methodists, Presbyterians, Episcopalians, Lutherans, and other "mainliners" who secretly whisper, "Thank God for the Baptists and Catholics." These mainline saints know that the public squabbles of their beleaguered Baptist and Catholic friends are keeping the spotlight off their own internal wrangles—at least for the moment.

And then there are the rest of us, beset by almost every conceivable kind of public and private pain.

We all hang by a tiny, tender, slender thread of grace.

But lo, a frightening mystery: though that fragile thread is stout beyond our understanding and its ways beyond our imagining, the Creator has seen fit to place the *stewardship* of that grace in our hands!

Ponder that if you want to lose some sleep.

What mean such things?

They mean we are faced with a choice: either to be bearers of grace or "buriers" of grace; either to be good, or bad, stewards of grace; either to support or not support one another.

To acknowledge that we all are human, that we all stumble and fall and that those of us who happen to be standing at the moment have a duty to lift up those of us who happen to have fallen at the moment—to acknowledge our common frailty is to open all of us to the mysterious miracles of grace.

For religious groups in strife, grace means that somehow the struggle becomes an opportunity for growth, that pain and suffering become the stuff from which redemption and reconciliation are forged. Grace finds a way.

So, hug a Baptist or a Catholic today. And if you can't find one of those, surely there's someone else nearby who needs your shoulder.

Walking Around an Old Question

It's an old question and it's one that can be either an arrogant presumption or an honest, if forthright, inquiry motivated by genuine concern: "Is it well with thy soul?"

It's the kind of question, in the kind of language, that one doesn't hear too often in today's sophisticated, secular society. There are reasons for that, some good and some bad.

More often than not, the question is asked by someone who is out to save somebody else's soul—singlehandedly and whether or not the poor, unsuspecting candidate *wants* his or her soul saved (or even acknowledges the concepts of soul and salvation)! God must have sweet compensations in store for those who are put upon in such ways.

Also, the question is rare these days because it is seen to be not only an impertinent intrusion into what many people rightly consider their own business, but also as doing violence to the highest spirit of biblical religion.

In what ways? First, because excessive concern for one's own spiritual welfare, represented by anxious fretting over the salvation of one's soul, is *essential selfishness*. And worse, it is *ultimate faithlessness*, a suggestion that God cannot be trusted to do, unbadgered, what He wants to do eagerly and of His own will.

Second, the question perpetuates the unbiblical notion that true religion is pie-in-the-sky-bye-and-bye stuff. And third, it implies private knowledge of the secret mind of God; it suggests that the individual who asks the question *knows*—perhaps exclusively!—what wellness of soul actually is.

The kind of religion associated with the question suggests that faith's main business is to provide a self-centered peace (even though others are suffering), assure abundant material blessings, and give special protection from life's hardships.

The biblical story, to the contrary, reveals something quite different: God's called and chosen people, rather than being selected for favor or honor, are to be servants (even suffering servants) of others. Their symbols are an exile and a cross. They are to be washers of feet, turners of cheeks, givers and not getters.

Wellness of soul in the biblical story is not so much a nebulous spirit that is "saved" as it is a specific life that is "given," a willingness to venture, to risk, to give all on behalf of others. Biblical faith is a life-stance which, rather than asking, "Is it well with thy soul?" invites the faithful to ask themselves, "Is it well with my neighbor? Is it well with the poor? With the powerless? With the hungry? With the imprisoned? With those denied justice and human rights?"

All the above having been said, it remains, however, that there is an imperishable rightness in the ancient question. Properly understood, it is one of *the* priority questions—not to be asked of others, but for individuals and nations to address to themselves.

The question, if obscure, is an ultimate one—which probably is the principal reason it isn't discussed in polite circles. Comfortable people don't like to be confronted with ultimate questions. Such questions disturb us. They lay claims upon us. They require change. They invite risk.

We may, for a time, evade the ultimate questions. What we cannot do, finally, is to escape them.

"We Love Our Son"

"We love our son John and will of course stand by him. Our hearts and prayers go out to the victims and their loved ones."

Those words from the parents of John Warnock Hinckley, Jr., the 25-year-old man who was apprehended in connection with last Monday's tragic shooting at Washington [an assassination attempt on President Ronald Reagan], invite us to examine a dimension of that event that is not likely to be addressed in popular comment. It is a dimension that is present whenever tragic crimes are committed: the agony experienced by the family and loved ones of those who commit criminal acts.

In a real sense, those persons, too, are very much among the victims of such acts. They experience pain and remorse every bit as great as, if not greater than, if they themselves were the primary targets.

It is an interesting commentary on our society that persons who suggest consideration of this dimension of the subject feel compelled to make some kind of explanation, some disclaimer, for that suggestion. Such a disclaimer would insist that compassion toward the parents in no way indicates any less sympathy for the primary victims; that it in no way implies any less anger that such things happen or any less frustration over living in a world that produced such tragedies.

Such a suggestion is an attempt, rather, to call attention to what is an often neglected attitude, even in a civilized society deeply influenced by Judeo-Christian sensitivities: compassion for *all* victims of life's tragedies; even—or perhaps especially—for its "unpopular" victims.

As will be the case with the shooting's primary victims and their families, life can never be the same for the parents and family of John Warnock Hinckley, Jr. Whatever solace may come from faith and from loyal and compassionate friends, history has its unrelenting way of perpetuating the nightmare experienced by such victims. Perhaps few tests of a human society are as great as the way it deals with its wounded, hurt "secondary victims" of tragedy.

The Hinckleys' pain is the pain of being parents, the pain of loving. Though not necessarily greater than that experienced by others who are hurt, it is a heavy, "special" kind of pain, the kind the Judeo-Christian tradition maintains that God knows most intimately. It is a pain that breaks the heart, an anguish that seems unbearable. Its bearers yearn that oneself, rather than one's loved one, were the primary sufferer.

The Hinckleys' pain is the kind of pain that lays a claim on all humanity, for all are either parent or child. It is, in the most real sense, a common pain; it calls us to bear one another's burdens.

While praying people remember President Reagan and the other primary victims in this tragedy, it is right and proper that prayers also be offered for John Warnock Hinckley, Jr., and, in a special way, for his anguished family.

By affirming, in the opening words of their first public statement, their love for their son John, the elder Hinckleys remind the rest of us that it is in such an attitude, and not through vengeance and retribution, that the way is to be found.

That's Too Long

It occurred to us the other day that it's been several weeks, yea months, since the word s-p-r-i-n-g has appeared in this column.

That's too long.

We submit that it would be an inexcusable oversight, perhaps some sort of sin, to let another day pass without paying due respect to that fairest of all seasons, you-know-what.

And besides, if we wait too long to say nice things about—that season—it'll be summer and hot and our tempers will be short and all we'll be able to think about is fall and winter and snow and then, before long, it'll be that season-that-comes-after-winter again and we'll have gone through the whole year without saying anything nice about that-time-of-the-year.

Whoa.

Come to think of it, there are lots of things, aside from—that season—that receive far too little attention from us mortals.

Like, for instance, fried okra. And grandchildren. And bicycles. And spouses.

Spouses for sure.

How long has it been since you sidled up to your spouse and told him/her how much you appreciate him/her?

That's too long.

There are lots of things we humans wait too long to do. Most of us would do well to examine our blind spots, our tendency to overlook those matters that deserve attention but which, for one reason or another, we neglect.

Today's sermonette allows for only a few for-instances.

■How long has it been, for instance, since you did something specific to counteract the bits of bigotry—if any amount of bigotry can be characterized as a "bit"—that continue to crop up here and there in Arkansas and throughout the country?

That's a long time.

■How long has it been since you responded to the loneliness of a friend, the fears of a child, the sensitivities of a teenager, or the hurts of a loved one?

See, we told you. As can happen with not saying nice things about s-p-r-i-n-g, there's such a thing as waiting too long to do the truly important things in life.

That really can be too long.

To Speak of Duty

We shall speak today of duty.

(Did we lose our audience?)

Duty. It is a noble, if unpopular, word. "Duty: a moral or legal obligation; an assigned service or responsibility; conduct due to others."

Duty. Responsibility. Obligation. Service.

Heavy words, indeed, guaranteed to chase many away.

"Speak to me not of duty," we fun-lovers say. "Speak rather of pleasure and happiness and leisure and license. Take your duty and peddle it elsewhere."

So it goes. But sometime, somewhere, someone must speak of duty.

Duty, of course, has many names. One person's duty is another's "petty obsession." One's duty is another's impertinence.

To nominate something to duty status is to start an argument.

"It is our duty to oppose abortion." "It is our duty to protect the inalienable right to make decisions regarding one's own body."

"It is our duty not to pollute our neighbors' airspace with poisonous tobacco smoke and to keep drinking drivers off the roads." "It is our duty to protect personal freedoms, including those to smoke and drink."

"It is our duty to guard innocent children from the ravages of pornography." "It is our duty to fight censorship."

And so on. Duty has many lovers, few students, fewer servants.

But there are, we contend, some indisputable duties held in common by followers of the biblical religions. Those duties:

■To be a faith-full people in an age when keeping faith

70

is a seemingly impossible feat.

■To be proclaimers of hope in a time when even the saints despair.

■To be seers of beauty and joy in a world where wonder often is crushed by human greed.

■To be encouragers of one's fellow human beings.

■To be strugglers toward love, pointers toward the way even though one may stumble awkwardly along the path.

■To be, however frail and unfit, keepers of dreams and custodians of visions.

■To be bringers of light, however small, into dark places, however large.

An old admonition remains: there's a duty to be fulfilled, little children of light. Go forth and shine.

On Hold for Dr. Bigpreacher

"Will you please hold for Dr. Bigpreacher?"

About 25 minutes pass, during which I'm subjected to recorded organ music, all sixteen verses of "I Come to the Garden Alone." What's Dr. Bigpreacher doing all this time? Writing a sermon? Meeting with the building committee? Does he really think I want to hear sixteen verses of "Garden"?

To the Garden Alone

Knowing I had to speak to the garden club in less than half an hour, I made the rounds of this paper's feature section the other morning in a desperate attempt to get some last-minute help. I needed a funny story to tell to the good ladies at the garden club brunch meeting.

I should have known better. Newsrooms are not your best place to go asking for stories you can tell at garden club meetings. There were several offers, not one of which could be reported in front of anybody's club of any kind.

About the only help—such as it was—that was offered came from a sympathetic soul who, sometime in his life, must have had the challenge of speaking to a garden club. "Are you going alone?" asked my friend the Arkansas Traveler.

"Yep. All by myself," I responded. "I'm tough."

"Well, maybe you could ask the girls if you could sing just one verse of that old favorite, 'I come to the garden club alone.'"

He didn't even smile when he said it.

After grimacing, I thanked my friend and rushed off to my meeting. Thinking it over on the way, I decided the Traveler's idea didn't sound so bad. I would try it—or at least would report his suggestion (not actually do the singing, heaven forbid).

Lo and behold, it worked! The nice ladies entered grandly into the moment, some laughing with proper restraint, some smiling politely, some waiting a few minutes and then giggling a bit. All garden club ladies are nice, I've learned, and marvelously sympathetic to the plight of a visiting speaker.

I owe one to the Traveler—and to my new friends in the garden club.

The occasion brings to mind that age-old problem: the

right thing to say at the right moment. That's a toughie. Few people, we suspect, have mastered the art—though it often appears a bunch think they have.

For what it's worth, the thought calls to mind an array of motherly admonitions that have survived the years. Perhaps it won't hurt to offer a few in the interest of better human relations throughout the universe:

Think before you speak. If you can't say something nice about somebody, don't say anything at all. Put your brain in motion before you put your mouth in gear. Don't never say nothin' nasty 'bout nobody.

If on the outside chance the occasion calls for brutal honesty, remember the biblical admonition (surely one of the most abused by self-interest): speak the truth in love. It takes a saint to do that without being hypocritical.

And, oh yes, remember. When you stand up to make your next speech and everybody laughs at you, don't take that stuff. Tell them you know a fellow who has friends in a garden club where they're real nice to guest speakers. So there.

Enough Is Enough

I wasn't going to say anything more about this, but enough is enough.

It happened again. This time on national television.

There I was, sitting in my own home at my own breakfast table finishing my grapefruit and Heartland Natural Cereal With No Added Preservatives when a "Today Show" commentator 'splained why Senator Alan Cranston fared so poorly in the Iowa primary.

"Let's face it," the New York expert said. "He's bald."

What's this? Senator Alan Cranston fared so poorly in the Iowa primary *because he's bald?*

That did it.

Have these eastern media people no sensitivity? No shame? I hadn't fully recovered from a similar trauma of some months before when a little penlight battery radio in my 20-year-old Volkswagen beetle told me—again in a Yankee accent (from a commentator who sounded like he had a head full of hair)—that "never again will a bald-headed man be president of the United States."

Humph.

How much are all you baldheaded people out there supposed to take?

It's time to call the hand of those who discriminate against the bald. It's time to infuse some religion into this debate.

■"Cut off thy hair, O Jerusalem, and cast it away...." (Jeremiah 7:29) Moral: Baldheaded men are more biblically obedient than hairy men.

■"Insurmountable evils have compassed about .... They are more than the hairs of mine head." (Psalm 40:12) Lesson: Fewer hairs, fewer evils. It followeth, therefore, that baldheaded men are more holy than hairy men.

■" ... [F]or man looketh on the outward appearance, but the Lord looketh on the heart." (I Samuel 16:7) Ah ha!

■"He that speaketh ill of his brother who is bald shall not inherit the Kingdom of Heaven." (Fourth John 106:98) I once had a neighbor who used to say about such dandy quotes, "If that's not in the Bible, it ought to be."

Now for the rest of the sermon, complete with your traditional three points and a poem:

One: A lot of baldheaded people have done a whole bunch of nice things on this earth.

Two: Many of those baldheaded people were Democrats. A few were even Republicans.

Three: God knows that baldheaded men are sorry for that sin and are, therefore, forgiven.

Poem: "There once was a man who was bald. He was gallant and completely without gall. He confessed his sin, was welcomed within, and shouted, 'Let there be good will to all!'"

Conclusion: it's no shame to have hair all over the top of your head. But don't blame God for being more pleased with those who don't conceal their countenance with a lot of messy, stringy stuff.

All God's children, however, may take heart. The Creator forgives all kinds of sins. Even hairiness.

Judgment Day Tips

I see that a media expert has given counsel on how to survive while being grilled by a television interviewer. The advice is timely, the expert notes, because with the rapidly growing number of low-power neighborhood television stations more people than ever soon will be facing the trauma of television interviews.

Such interviews, the media man says, are experiences that cause giants to quake.

And well they should.

The topic suggests another experience designed to make giants quake: that Ultimate Interview—the one that even more people are certain to face: the Judgment Day grilling by the Big Interviewer in the Sky.

With apologies to the media expert, we adapt some of his helpful tips for use in preparing for that fateful confrontation.

■Project a friendly, relaxed presence and use a conversational tone of voice. Be nice. The Interviewer's first response will be emotional rather than intellectual, so remember that first impressions are important. If you have any doubts about yourself, these will be communicated. What's said in these sessions is rarely remembered; how you look is.

■Be aware of your body language when reacting to questions. If you look skyward before answering a question, you may seem to be asking for divine guidance. Remember where you are—look straight ahead.

■Forget the "no comment" response. In some places that's okay, but not here. The Interviewer knows all about you anyway.

■If you feel the interview is going in a direction you don't want to follow, redirect the conversation by saying, "But there was this good deed I did back in 1954 ..."

■Let the Interviewer have the appearance of being in charge of things, but keep control in your own hands. You won't get the last word, but make sure the ones you do get count.

■If the Interviewer starts quoting scripture and says something like, "Man looketh on the outward appearance but God looketh on the heart, I Samuel 16:7," be nice. But then go into your best Phil Donahue "one, two, three, kick-'em-in-the-teeth" routine: "Hey, Man, this is the real world. What are you talkin' about!"

Bumper Sticker Theology

Sermons are where you find them—even on automobile bumpers. Consider a few homiletic offerings observed recently (with brief after-service commentary at no extra charge):

■*God Said It, I Believe It, That Settles It.* (No beating around the bush there.)

■*Three Things That Made This Country Great: God, Guns, and Guts.* (More straightforward sermonizing here—doesn't leave you wondering where that chap's coming from.)

■*Christians Aren't Perfect, Just Forgiven.* (Not bad theology.)

■*In the Event of the Rapture, This Vehicle Will Be Unat-*

tended. (Humility will be addressed in a later sermon.)
■*If You Love Jesus, Tithe.* (It beats honking.)
■*Bloom Where You're Planted.* (Nice.)
■*God Is My Co-Pilot.* (This driver was speeding and made an illegal left turn. One would assume the Co-Pilot was off-duty.)
■*Praise the Lord Anyway.* (Nice thought. That would look good on my 20-year-old Volkswagen beetle.)
■*Love Your Neighbor—Jesus Does.* (Good preachin'.)
■*Another Student for Christ.* (Hope he doesn't get caught praying in class.)
■*Christians' Retirement Is Good.* (The facilities are nice.)
■*Heaven or Hell—Turn or Burn.* (In seminary that's called "preaching for a decision.")
■*Hallelujah!* (Me, too—a good all-'round reaction.)

Freedom of religious expression is one of the grand treasures of this country, of course, and to all their own in this respect. But as far as preaching goes, bumper sticker theology raises that always popular question, "Just what *is* a good sermon, anyway?"

In spite of the fact that you've probably already discussed this topic with three friends this week, we suggest there may be more to say on the subject. Therefore, we offer the following additional commentary.

Sermons, one is tempted to say, are better demonstrated than heard—or read. "I'd rather see a sermon *lived* than speeding by at 60 miles per hour." "The best sermon is one that *breathes.*"

Having said such things, it remains, one supposes, that there's a place for bumper sticker sermonizing. Those little strips do enable people to declare themselves. And it's just possible that they could help someone. One could wish, however, that so many of the stickers weren't in such bad taste that they detract from the *essential dignity* of religious witness.

But on reflection, some religious bumper stickers do qualify as pragmatic theology. Consider another seen recently: *Hell Needs No Reservations.* Just think of all the long-distance phone calls that one will save!

Gospel Telephone

The following is an open letter to this country's clergy:

Dear Reverend Sir (or Reverend Madam):

I know you're a busy person, so please pardon this intrusion. But I've got a complaint about your telephone manners. (Please hold for a moment while I answer my "call waiting" signal. Thanks.

Back now—sorry to be so long.)

It's this problem, see, with telephone etiquette. Not that it's anything real big, but it is a bit annoying. I only bring it up because some folks out there may be really put off by such little things. I'm trying to be helpful. Honest.

Let's take the problems one at a time:

■There's the "Will you please hold for Dr. So-and-so" routine. It's not any big deal, but it is a bit irritating. It goes something like this:

The telephone rings and I answer. "Hello?"

A secretary inquires, "Mr. Workman?"

"Speaking."

"Will you please hold for Dr. Bigpreacher?"

About 25 minutes pass, during which I'm subjected to recorded organ music, all sixteen verses of "I Come to the Garden Alone." What's Dr. Bigpreacher doing all this time? Writing a sermon? Meeting with the building committee? Does he really think I want to hear sixteen verses of "Garden"?

(I confess to sin: After being asked to "hold for Dr. Bigpreacher," when he finally comes on the line I'm tempted to fake a secretary's voice and say, "Mr. Bigpreacher? Will you please hold for Dr. Workman?" But that wouldn't be nice, so naturally I don't do it.)

Finally, Dr. Bigpreacher (whom I've never met) comes on the line: "Good morning, John! It's a beautiful day the Lord has made, isn't it?"

How am I expected to respond to that? I am closed in here in my cubicle, can't see out the window, am rushing to meet a deadline, and now I can't get "I Come to the Garden Alone" out of my mind. I'm tempted to say something like, "Well, it started off pretty well," but I don't. I mustn't embarrass my employer so I respond in kind, mumbling something that sounds like an echo of Dr. Bigpreacher's greeting.

■Then there's your basic "call waiting" situation. You're right at the critical point in your conversation when that "click-click" is heard and your caller says, "Pardon me a moment, I've got to get this other call." Most people are fairly thoughtful about such things and get back to you as soon as possible. But for us folks with sensitive psyches, it's pretty crushing to be informed so abruptly that you're being demoted to second place. It's such a small thing, of course, but I thought you ought to know.

■Then there's the instance, quite rare, I'll admit, in which a pastor has an unlisted telephone number that his secretary refuses to disclose. What if I were in desperate need of spiritual counseling? Or wanted to give him a love offering of three billion bucks?

There's something about shepherds of the flock having unlisted telephone numbers that just doesn't square theologically.

I know there're more important things to be concerned about these days than telephone manners. But it could be that such little things are symbols of more important matters—that they say something about preachers being servants of humanity rather than Madison Avenue business tycoons.

If all this seems too caustic, forgive me and blame it on my having had a bad day on the telephone. I'm really on your side and would like to be of help.

Yours for more effective reaching out and touching,

J.S.W.

A Talk with God

It being popular these days to talk with God in private and report about it in public, we thought we'd get on the bandwagon. Here goes.

We talked with God the other day, and God told us exactly how to vote in the upcoming election.

That's right. Not only did God tell us how to vote on each of the four proposed amendments to the state constitution, God also told us God's choice in the races for governor, senator, congress, and whatever ("My G-team," God said to us with a laugh).

But that's not all.

Even without our asking, God proceeded to tell us God's thoughts on tax reform, the national budget deficit, and foreign policy ("with special reference to Central America," God said with an audible wink).

And there's more. God told us a couple of other things we'd always wondered about but were afraid to ask.

So here we are, fresh from a conversation with God, and a whole column to report it. Oh, boy.

Only there's a problem.

God told us not to tell anyone what God said about the most important things we discussed. God said that much of our conversation was confidential—"Top sacred stuff," God said, again with that laugh.

We agreed, of course, to keep our silence. Sorry.

There are some things, though, that God said we *had* to tell you or God would never talk to us again.

God said you weren't going to like this one bit and we told God that that wasn't the half of it. We also told God to stick around and get us out of this, just in case. But God said for us to go ahead anyway: so here goes.

First, God said to tell all you people that if you don't "quit sinning and start living right" (God's words, not ours), then ... (God told us not to disclose the rest of it).

Second, God said to tell you folks that there's good news and bad news about all that end-of-the-world talk from our prophets of doom. The good news, God said, is that they're only partially right. The bad news, God said, is that they didn't even get close to it.

Third, God said for us to tell all you politicians to keep praying but to "pray right" and that, in God's own words, "you'd better get this straight: *God doesn't like prayers used for partisan political purposes!*" (Emphasis God's.)

And oh, yes. God said to tell all of you to quit blaming God for the flooding of the Arkansas River.

(Personally, we weren't too impressed by God's reasoning on this one—a bunch of clichés about the just and the unjust, that sort of thing.)

And of course God, being God, had to close the conversation with religious talk.

God said that whatever else we reported, to be sure to tell you folks to keep your chin up. That's exactly what God said. Keep your chin up, love life, and get out there and do some good.

Bound to Happen

It was bound to happen. A national religion test is in the offing.

It could have been predicted. It was just a matter of time.

According to our informants, it hasn't been determined who will be required to take the test—whether preachers, political candidates, air traffic controllers, babysitters, or whoever. But public officials already are pushing forward, eager to be first to be declared religiously orthodox.

To find out more about this insidious scheme, we sent one of our crack investigative reporters to pose as a religion test-taker.

"I'm here to take the religion test," our man, understandably nervous, said to the federal religion examiner.

"Relax," the examiner replied. "It's a snap. No bottles—nothing like that."

"Then how do you test for religious orthodoxy?" our man asked.

"We've developed our own surefire test," the examiner said. "First, there's the written part. You answer questions—like things about God and sin and heaven and hell, stuff like that. Then there's the handshake part."

"The handshake part?" our man asked.

"Yep," the examiner replied. "If you flunk the written test you can be approved if you pass the handshake test."

The examiner continued. "The handshake test was developed by a panel of experts from the world's nine major religions. Our agents have been trained to identify religious orthodoxy by the way a person shakes hands."

"Amazing," our undercover reporter responded, conscious that his palms were sweating. "And if that fails?"

"If that fails, our people have the option of applying the 'voice sincerity test.' That's simple, too. We just ask the person to recite a phrase—a verse of scripture or a line of a hymn, something like that—and, by a formula devised by our experts, we can tell if the person is really orthodox."

"Really orthodox?" our man asked.

"Sure. Really orthodox. You know, like believing all the right things and stuff like that. You know, being sincere."

"Oh, yes," our man said. "Of course."

To return to reality, we're reasonably sure we're safe

from any such religion test. At least we think we are.

On the other hand, one could argue that there's always been a lot of religion testing going on. Whether it's the religious right imposing its views through partisan political structures, or the subtle judgments that many religious people unconsciously impose on persons of other faiths, religious testing—also known as religious bigotry—is an odious fact of life.

If a test for orthodoxy is difficult to devise, a test for bigotry is easy: do we judge others on the basis of whether they believe as we do, or whether they "dislike the same people" we do, or whether they worship on the "correct" day of the week and don't wear funny religious garb? And so on.

But it's nice that we don't have to worry about such things around here.

The Big One

It's about time that this newspaper's Religion Department had another staff meeting. According to our Agenda Committee, we're long overdue in dealing with some big issues.

(The last time our people got together we ended up designating our six-by-eight cubicle a Nuclear-Free Zone, the first such site, we believe, in midtown Little Rock. We were second, locally, only to west Little Rock's Unitarian Church in making such a public declaration.)

Now, it appears, our folks are restless again.

"There's lots of mumblin' going on out there," our department personnel manager said the other day. "These people are edgy."

What's the problem, we asked.

"It's different this time, boss. It seems it's the big one."

"The big one?"

"Yep, the big one. Spiritual burnout. These people are showin' some frightening symptoms. They play more golf, sit on the back row and grumble during department meetings, are generally negative all the time. It's serious."

Oh my sakes. Burnout. Not here, we thought.

There's more, according to another staff member.

"There's compassion fatigue out there, chief," this mid-level executive in our Protestant Department said. "Just the other day one of our most faithful writers was heard to mumble 'Who cares?' when told of yet another alarming report of this country's declining moral health."

And that's not all. The head of our Eastern Religions Division was actually heard to say 'So what?' when someone reported increased violence among religious sects in India.

And so it went, report after report of the heartbreak of spiritual burnout, right here in our own department.

We mused a moment, remembering that just the other day we heard a preacher tell a bunch of other preachers that they didn't have anyone but themselves to blame for spiritual burnout.

Humph. That preacher was from Texas, we remembered, so what did he know.

That same day we heard another Texas preacher who had the presumption to remind that same group of Arkansas reverends that the gospel itself claims to be foolishness (he cited chapter and verse) and that so long as those preachers chose to proclaim such things, they could expect to get burned.

Humph again.

But those two Texas preachers, broad-brimmed hats and all, had some more to say. They talked about something called the "grace of God," which, they said, was able to take care of folks like us—burned out or fired up or whatever—in days like these. It's funny. It sounds like they may have heard the Good News even down there in Texas. We told all this to our Religion Department people the other day, and they said they felt better immediately.

River City Crisis

What we got on our hands, right here in River City, is a crisis. A real-life, full-blown spiritual crisis.

Somebody is stealing Bibles from the *Gazette*.

(Yes, the *Gazette* has Bibles—or did before the fabled and feared Dreaded Bible Bandit [DBB] started doing his thing.)

It's your classic good-news-bad-news story. The good news is that a genuine revival of religion must be about to break out around here. The bad news is that somebody's stealing our Bibles to make it happen.

It's a small price, I suppose.

It all started some months ago when my Revised Standard Version, one of two Bibles I had in my cubicle, was borrowed, never to be seen again. Assorted Bible reference books soon followed and just the other day the DBB struck again, this time goin' for the gold: he (or she—let's not be prejudiced here) took my King James Version, with concordance and maps!

Has this DBB person no shame?

I was reduced to having to go to our *Gazette* library to request the loan of one of our company Bibles. But lo and behold, the DBB had penetrated even our fail-safe Library Bible Security System and absconded with all our KJVs and other versions, leaving only one of those insipid contemporary translations that doesn't have a single "ye" or "thou" or "begat" in the whole thing.

We're talkin' crisis here.

My search—I was getting desperate by this time—took me to the rarefied atmosphere of our much-reverenced Third Floor, where our editorial writers pace to and fro contemplating eternal truth and stuff. Bible reading and quoting is such a common Third Floor pastime I knew there'd be Good Books there to spare.

I was not disappointed. Our elevated elders were more than happy to share the Word. "Use mine, my child," they pled devoutly, yea righteously.

This epidemic of Biblenapping worries me. Don't get me wrong. I'm all for propagating the Word. I just don't like to have it stolen. I'd gladly give my Bible to anyone in need. (I'm not so sure, however, about those expensive resource books. It might be that someone's soul could be saved by reading *The Handbook of Denominations in the United States, 1981,* but I've yet to hear of it.)

Oh, well. On the small chance that the DBB may be reading this column, I suggest a few passages for extended meditation: Genesis 31:27; Exodus 20:15; Leviticus 19:11; Zachariah 5:3; and Ephesians 4:28.

Oh, yes—remember also that venerable passage (quoted here by memory from the new Inclusive Language Lectionary), "He/she who taketh his/her brother's Bible without permission is condemned to spend two weeks in the hot place or one week in Texas."

Go ye therefore and don't do likewise.

In the meantime, share some Good News with others. Somebody may have run off with all their Bibles.

A Preacher Testing Law?

Word comes that there's a movement afoot to enact a statewide preacher testing law.

Hmmm.

According to our sources, a bunch of denominational executives have become so exercised over what they consider the sad state of this country's religious life that they're determined to go to the source.

"It's the preachers!" one righteously indignant executive is reported to have exclaimed. "Let's test 'em!"

It seems a committee was named to solicit sentiment among the saints regarding how they felt about their preachers. An unknown source silently slipped a supply of such sentiments, suitably signed by the submitters, under our door the other day and we herewith share a sampling of the same:

■From Pew-Weary in Prescott: "We want our preacher-boys to say it fast and tell it plain! 'Tain't no 'scuse fer no preacher to preach more'n one hour. Remember three points and a poem are enough and no souls are saved past noon!"

■From Got It Right in Gurdon: "Absolutely do not unleash on the unsuspecting public any preacher who: (1) has been to the Holy Land; (2) has attended seminary; or (3) has an honorary doctor's degree."

■From Doctrinally Bold in Bald Knob: "Make sure they passed 'Rapture' in seminary and didn't take no Greek nor Hebrew."

■From Had Too Much in Hot Springs: "Don't never license no preacher 'lessen he [only one writer indicated a preacher could be a 'she'] solemnly swears not to hold more'n two meetin's a week! By the time one goes to choir practice and prayer meetin' and circle it's all a body can stand."

■From Theologically True in Texarkana: "Test 'em on

practical theology. Can they baptize a 300-pound convert in a two-foot creek?"

■From Busy All the Time in Bauxite: "Check the wife. Can she pray in public and play the piano by ear?"

There's more, but we've been advised that the deacons are going to act soon on this proposal and don't want the brothers and sisters to become too agitated.

In the meantime, let your preacher know how much you appreciate him or her. Preachers are a much-hounded species these days and could use a generous portion of understanding, compassion, and support.

Have you hugged your preacher today?

Word Has Come

We're reluctant to mention this, but word has come that a couple of reverends have been caught cheating on the exam required by the new statewide Preacher Testing Law.

It's a shame, of course, and we report this regrettable episode only in the interest of the public's right to know.

"If gold rusts, what will iron do?" one outraged parishioner is reported to have exclaimed.

"Humph," another said. "If you can't trust your preacher, who can you trust?"

"But what can you expect when they're paid so poorly?" yet another sister, this one more benevolent, moaned.

There has, in fact, been a lot of bemoaning the episode, the news of which came to us from an informant who asked not to be identified.

Chief among the bemoaners have been denominational officials and representatives of the Preachers' Union. To a person, those officials insist the offending were few in number and in no way representative of the profession.

"There's a bad apple in every barrel—just ask Eve," one longtime preacher-observer quipped during an interview. "But that doesn't mean you throw out the whole barrel, now does it."

Well, hardly, we said, trying to look innocent.

There's talk of a State Police investigation of the episode, though one cleric said that might precipitate a touchy church/state entanglement. The tests, stored in the choir room of a Baptist church in Izard County and guarded by an off-duty election official, were thought to be secure and tamperproof.

But whatever, the event illustrates an age-old problem, one to which the Scriptures speak: what to make of it when good people sin.

An old Pentecostal preacher from Stone County called us the other day and said he just wanted to remind us, "before you say too much about that preacher-cheatin' stuff," to remember the Old Testament story about the Lord keeping faith in the whole human race even if only a handful of righteous persons could be found throughout the whole land.

"Now think about that for a while," he said. "Isn't that just like God?"

Yes, we said, we suppose it is.

We promised we'd think about it.

Good Times and Tears

No more sharing socks from Dad's drawer. No more lying awake after midnight wondering what time he'll be home. No more high school dances. Or having to share the car. No more sitting together in the church pew on Sunday morning. And now the ghosts that fill our house, silent these many years, will have their day.

Golden Day in the Sun

It was a beautiful day, one of the few sunny, rain-free Sunday afternoons we've had in recent weeks, a lovely, lazy hint of summer days to come. My five-year-old grandson and I were in the back yard at his house, playing. We'd swing, slide down the slide, and take turns kicking the big yellow-green plastic ball around the yard. Much fun, much laughing. A golden day in the sun.

Mom and Dad and sister Jenny and Aunt Susie and Grandmother were inside the house, visiting.

During a break between games, my grandson paused, the light of a marvelous idea suddenly upon his face. "I know what we can do! Why don't we go in and tell everybody to come out here—and we can ... we can ... we can all just enjoy the day!"

It was, of course, the kind of remark that makes grandparents smile. But I submit it was something more than a cute comment, that it was something not so much to be laughed about by adults as to be rejoiced at, lingered over, smiled at knowingly, and warmly tucked away in memory's treasurehouse.

Even with a grandfather's license, I submit that the remark reflects one of those rare and beautiful golden moments in life, one of those fleeting yet elegant vignettes of discovery that makes human beings such marvelous creatures. Such moments provide fleeting glimpses into the beauty and mystery of existence. They are priceless moments when one is afforded a vision of the grandeur and wonder of life.

In a moment, a secret of the universe is revealed in a back yard in Van Buren, Arkansas.

Too grand a claim for a child's comment?

I think not. Jesus spoke of the reality: "Unless you become as little children...."

The experience recalls a similar happening of some fifteen or so years ago, now a favorite in our scrapbook of family stories. I had taken our youngest of four children, then about four years old, with me to the automatic car wash. I prepared him for what was to happen—Daddy would put a quarter into that machine and drive the car inside that funny-looking building, and then a lot of water would shoot against the car and big brushes would wash off the dirt.

Our young son took it all in with looks of astonishment and wonder. When our 25 cents was used up, he responded with unbridled joy, "Oh boy—maybe next time we can bring the whole family!"

Precisely. Good times are to be shared, enjoyed by those one loves.

We live in difficult and trying days, time not especially designed to enable one always to "enjoy the day." But little children have a special gift for such times. They remind us that there is, after all, so much about life to be enjoyed.

Take it from an authority, my grandson: while you have opportunity, enjoy the day with those you love.

Vacation Report

There ought to be a law against people talking about their vacations. However, since no such statute exists (at least yet), I'd like to get in a few quick remarks.

I currently am in the fifth day of my vacation. And, since I'm in a hurry to get back to resting up, this won't take a lot of time. It shouldn't hurt too much.

During the last 120 hours I have spent an enormous amount of time in close proximity to most of the members of my immediate family plus a considerable number of other loved ones and friends. In my case (pardon all the personal references), immediate family means my wife, our four children, one daughter-in-law, one son-in-law, two grandchildren, two sets of parents, two sets of in-laws, and one (for want of a better word) grandhorse, a colt recently born to a mare belonging to our daughter and son-in-law.

Please don't misunderstand me. I love my family and my in-laws and I like being with them and with all those other people I've had close communion with since I took some time off to rest and relax and have fun. It's amazing how much resting and relaxing and fun-having one can do when there're so many people eager to help.

But, again, don't get me wrong. It's just that here I am with most of my vacation already gone, and I'm almost rested out.

However, I have, in just five days, been able to do a lot of vacation-type things. I have traveled. (We went to West Fork and Conway.) I have visited. (With all those people and animals noted above and several others.) I have looked at family pictures. (There have been at least two marathon film festivals plus numerous un-scheduled album and individual photo reviews.) I have played gang tennis. And I have supervised my three-and-a-half-year-old grandson while he learned to type perfectly on my electric typewriter and have rocked my five-month-old granddaughter while she cooed me to sleep.

But that's not all. I've found time to do a couple of the many things I had planned to accomplish during my vacation. I've shined my Sunday shoes and have been to Magic Mart to purchase two new flashlight batteries and four picture frames. And there's a good chance I'll get around to framing the four photos for which the frames have long been planned. All this achieved and I'm not even halfway through my vacation.

Mixed in with all this has been time for some reading and, though I've tried to avoid it, some thinking. As a matter of fact, when this column was first planned it was to contain some serious comments (some real gems) on weightier matters of the day.

But all that will have to wait. My grandson wants to use the typewriter now and my out-of-town family members are busy visiting in the den without me. They may even be about to look at some more pictures.

Thank You, P.S. Muckenfuss

You don't know P.S. Muckenfuss. You couldn't be expected to.

P.S. Muckenfuss is a horse, two-week-old first-born foal of Marty, an Arabian mare who belongs to our daughter and son-in-law. He is, you might say, our grandhorse.

Having two grandchildren already, I thought I had exhausted my excitement over such events. But the birth of P.S. Muckenfuss—"Fuss" for short—has renewed my spirits and refreshed my soul. One may be excused, perhaps, for carrying on about such things.

We first met Fuss a week ago, when he was just six days old. It was a beautiful day in the Ozark Mountains in northwest Arkansas when we joined the celebration to bring Fuss to the family. But even joyous occasions can being painful recollections.

I remember, Susie, although it's been fifteen years ago, that day I had to tell you that the long-awaited foal of your first little pony, Honeycomb, was stillborn. I recall how you cried, softly, bravely. And I remember my tears and those of our good neighbor, Mr. Thompson, who came early that morning to bring the sad news. I remember, too, the grave I dug at the far end of the pasture, covering your dreams with summer's soft brown sod.

Today, I could tell that behind that unconvincing mask of

six-day-old innocence, P.S. Muckenfuss knew all about that day ...

It's amazing how functional a week-old foal can be. Fuss would dart to and fro from one end of the corral to the other, taking off in a run, testing his spindly legs, surprising himself and us with jumps, and buck, all four little hooves in the air at the same time! What a wonder are the ways of God's creatures.

The summer wind blows strongly this afternoon, giving a good workout to the tall, stately trees around the corral. There is life in that wind, in those trees, in the way Marty protects her foal against these well-meaning celebrants. How interesting, too, that the only one Fuss will come to is our three-and-a-half-year-old grandson, John Thomas. Little children of all kinds seem to know something their elders long since have forgotten.

P.S. Muckenfuss. What kind of name is that? One would think that registered Arabian horses should have exotic names like Shiekh so-and-so or Abu-ben-somebody.

Our daughter tells us that P.S. is for her brother Paul Steven, on whose birthday Fuss was born, and that Muckenfuss is after a name found in the back of an old book in the U of A Law Library, where she works. (Also, as it was happily recalled later, the name has family connections. Susie's great-grandfather, while a student at Wofford College in South Carolina in the late 1800s, had three roommates. The four chaps could have formed a neat law firm of their own: Hiram, Buckram, Workman, and Muckenfuss. Had he been at Saturday's gathering, old Muckenfuss would have been pleased.)

Time to go now. One wonders what P.S. Muckenfuss, one of the newest descendants of the earliest residents of earth, thinks about what's happening in this tired old world and what we're doing to his planet. Does his advent, accompanied by kicking hooves and joyous outbursts of energy, have anything to do with vast pasturelands being threatened with conversion to mobile missile sites, with human inmates on death rows, with nerve gas factories, with escalating arms races?

Somehow, P.S. Muckenfuss and every other newborn crea-
ture in God's world have everything to do with such things!

Thank you, Fuss, for the secrets you shared last Saturday. We got your message. The dream must be kept
alive.

Good Times and Tears

It's not nice to push your personal life off on others,
but that's what I'm about to do. Next week my wife and I
begin what some might call a new chapter in our lives.
After 30 years of having children at home, the youngest
of our four goes away to college and, as the saying goes,
our nest will be empty.

The situation presents a perplexing instance of mixed
emotions. Should one be sad—or glad?

Both, I suspect. And both for good and healthy
reasons.

In our case, I'm not sure who's the more elated—our
young son or his weary parents. He's excited about the
prospect of being free, away from the burdens of family,
out on his own, and having new experiences. We're excited about the prospect of being free, away from the
burdens of family, out on our own, and having new
experiences.

Or, at least, we're all trying to convince ourselves that
that's the way we feel about it.

Actually, that's not the whole story. In spite of our
son's excitement at the prospects before him, I've
noticed that he, too, is actually beginning to mellow.
Last week, for no apparent reason, he actually kissed his
mother. And one evening the week before, I actually
refrained from delivering my usual stern lecture when

he came in later than "the regular time."

Thirty years on anybody's calendar is a long time. But if I've learned anything over the years approaching this watershed event, it's that the old-timers have been right all along: this time comes a whole lot faster than you think it will.

The song has it right: turn around, and your children are grown.

It's time for reflection. As I recall, there were at least two other major watersheds regarding my parental responsibilities and I survived them both: a dozen years or so ago when I gave my swan-song sex lectures; and a half-dozen years later when I completed my final "teach you to drive" course. After that I felt I was home free.

No more asking "How'd it go today, Chuck?" No more sharing socks from Dad's drawer. No more lying awake after midnight wondering what time he'll be home. No more high school dances. Or having to share the car. No more sitting together in the church pew on Sunday morning.

And now the ghosts that fill our house, silent these many years, will have their day. But that, too, will be a happy time. The photos of our four children—and now two grandchildren—will be there, calling forth memories that continually grow brighter. And there'll be telephone calls, of course, unpredicted surprises to lighten the day. And happy reunions will be planned, to be looked forward to.

But now that I'm entering this new era, I'm not really sure how to feel about it.

Glad, I think. Both for our children who can be on their own and for their parents who have all those wonderful memories to enjoy and others yet to come.

In many ways, it's a joyous time. But that doesn't mean that after I've made jokes about it, I can't shed a tear or two, does it?

The good times make for some of the best crying times.

[Editor's note: What follows is excerpted from an article written soon after "Good Times and Tears."]

"There are only two things you can give your children."
The dean of the university was speaking at the initial orientation session.
"Roots and wings."
We were all there in the university gym—freshmen students and parents, from places near and far. There was an atmosphere of mixed emotions, the excitement and uncertainty that accompany all new beginnings and the pain that goes with the cutting of ties.
"You can only give your children roots and wings."
What a marvelous insight, I thought. Its essential truth—and its glory and pain—struck something deep inside me. I was immensely moved.
I already had decided there was nothing to shed tears about as this time of parting came. It really was a happy occasion and joy was the only proper emotion.
But I have long known that joy is one of the most potent evokers of tears. And the occasion, climaxing not only the 18 years that our youngest had been preparing for this experience but also the 30 years during which we'd had our children at home, suddenly hit me, right there in far-off New Jersey where, among Yankees and strange-talking people, I was leaving my youngest son.
I thought at first that I could get by with the lump in my throat. But the roots and wings did it, unleashing emotions, grounded in decades, even generations, of histories, memories, associations, and ties. The tears came, irresistibly, silently.
It helped to know that other fathers and mothers throughout that university gymnasium were experiencing the same.
But the tears were ones of deep, abiding joy.
God be in the roots. God be in the wings.

Reflections on a Holiday Visit

Just about the time I get used to writing 1982, they go and change the year on me. It's always been that way, as I remember, but it gets worse as the years pile up. And according to a friend of mine who's really old, I can't expect it to get any better.

It's funny, the things old men think about when the years change. Mostly, I suppose, they think about when they were young. I don't really know this, of course—I'm just supposing. But I do notice that supposing is becoming easier these days.

I tried, the other evening, to think about something that happened when I was young, but I couldn't remember anything. So I settled for thinking about my grandchildren—John Thomas, who is almost five, and Jennifer, who is almost two.

The two, with their parents and assorted uncles and an aunt, graced our house for several days during this glad holiday season. The visit made me recall someone saying that grandchildren are so much fun one should have them first.

One rainy afternoon after Christmas Day, when playing with new toys had gotten a bit old, my grandson and I decided we'd make a tent. We went to an upstairs bedroom, got out the card table, spread a quilt over it, and crawled into our little camp home, which was in the woods, down by a stream.

I was enjoying it so much, after a hearty holiday meal, that I grabbed a pillow and volunteered to stand guard while John Thomas went out to hunt for bears.

There's a problem with this, though. It's doesn't take a five-year-old grandson long to find bears in a couple of upstairs bedrooms. Within minutes, just about the time I had traveled off to dreamland, John was back in camp with a couple of the biggest bears you've ever seen and wanting, now, to play with something else.

It was time, the young hunter said, to go back downstairs and play with the electric train. That'd be fun, now wouldn't it. Grandchildren, these days, are a whole lot more active than they used to be.

Now playing with an electric train is a sure way to forget that the years are marching on. Show me an older man who doesn't like to play with an electric train and I'll show you a really old man indeed. After several times around the track, however, even electric training can run its course.

"Now we can paint, Grandpaw!"

Only the cruelest Scrooge could say no to such an excited invitation. (Don't children ever sleep anymore?)

Painting, of course, is creative activity, the kind of thing during which, with each stroke of the brush, you can almost see little minds being formed in marvelous ways.

The trouble with being a grandfather helping your grandson paint is that you want to keep his nice red fuzzy pajama sleeves out of the paint. You might as well give up. It won't work. About the best thing you can do is to work out an agreement that after painting, it's time to go to bed.

That, I found, really worked. After we painted awhile, I went to bed. I think John Thomas stayed up for a couple of hours, having fun with Grandmaw.

As for me, I slept soundly, dreaming that I did not, after all, have to be so afraid for the future.

A Rose in Brooklyn

If all goes as planned, by the time these comments are printed I will have met for the first time my new seven-week-old granddaughter. She lives in Brooklyn, at New York City, where she was born—a fact that once and for all shatters the theory that nothing good can happen north of the Mason-Dixon line.

God can do good things up north. A rose grows in Brooklyn.

First meetings are old stuff, of course, to us 59-year-olds. Having been grandfathered twice already, we're totally prepare to take this third such first meeting in stride. No problems here. We're calm.

Furthermore, we long ago pledged to not commit one of those mushy "To My Granddaughter" pieces. No ask-me-about-my-granddaughter stuff for us. No siree. We're above that. Instead, we've decided to write one of those "To My Precious Granddaughter" pieces.

So, Julie, this is for you, though it's written a couple of days before the two of us will meet.

I suppose I ought to introduce myself (though your parents have probably already tried to do that).

I'm your grandfather, your father's daddy. (We Southerners call them "Daddy"—just one of the many odd things about us, as you'll learn.) Your cousins, also Southerners who talk funny, call me "Grandpaw." But you can call me whatever you want to. Even with a Yankee accent, "Grandpaw," "Grandfather," or whatever will sound wonderful.

I'm not going to embarrass both of us, Julie, by getting sentimental here or trying to say all those wise things that grandfathers attempt to come up with on such occasions. Nor am I going to speak of how frightening this world is, and all that. You'll learn such things soon enough.

Rather, Julie, let us, on our first meeting, talk together of beauty.

Beauty. It's a theme that I suppose you know more about than I do, really, though it's beyond you just now to speak of such things. You now live in that mysterious world we adults have lost forever that we can never re-capture. It's a world where everything is new, mysteri-ous, sometimes frightening, and, as you know but are unable to express, so truly beautiful.

So, Julie, if you could speak, I would sit quietly at your feet and let you talk to me of beauty. Do try, please, as best you can, to get across to us—this bunch of proud, even silly, adults, making so over you—your urgent messages fresh from the Creator's secret treasurehouse of wonders.

Speak to us, in your cryptic, wordless way, of marvel and mystery and joy. Speak to us of our need for each other. Speak to us of love.

We adults, Julie, too often pose as the wise ones. But, in truth, you are our teacher. We desperately need to learn from you, so recent a messenger from the great beyond.

Nap for awhile, if you must. We'll learn from you sleeping, too. And when you awake, we'll take up class again.

Together Again

The first thing Ol' Jim said was, "It sure has been a long winter, John."

"Yep," I answered. "It sure has."

Ol' Jim is my second-hand, seven-year-old, 25-dollar, only-had-two-flats, ten-speed bicycle, with whom I've shared many a good time. The other day's outing, one of the first of the season, was west on Markham Parkway on a delightfully sunny and warm Saturday afternoon.

"Looks like a dandy day, John," Ol' Jim said.

"Yep. Sure does."

(One of the nice things about traveling with Ol' Jim is that you don't have to worry about conversation. He does most of the talking and I do most of the listening. So far, we've both been satisfied with the arrangement. Occasionally, though, when Ol' Jim gets to talking too much I let him ramble on and on without any response. He soon gets the message. Once in awhile, though, he'll turn the tables on me. It was that way Saturday.)

"Look at that, Jim! That blackberry bush over yonder is a-bustin' out all over with blossoms! It's gonna be a grand summer ahead, yes siree. Just think of all them delicious berries we're gonna get this year!"

No response.

One would think, wouldn't one, that such excited comments would elicit an equally excited response. But no. Ol' Jim wouldn't say a word.

I let some time and a few miles pass before trying again. Ol' Jim seemed unnaturally quiet.

"Wow! Would ya lookit that! See all them honeysuckle bushes over there? And catch a whiff of that smell! The first honeysuckle of the season—there's nothin' like it!"

Still no response.

I started to ask what the problem was but thought better of it.

Four farms later, Jim finally spoke.

"John"—I could feel it; he was in his mood—"you're the one that gets to do all the berry eatin' and flower sniffin'. Why don't you think of me once in a while? That wouldn't hurt, now would it?"

Oh, no, I thought. Here we go again. It's going to be one of those kinds of summers.

"This is where we left off last fall, Jim, with you griping all the time about having to do all the work and never having any of the fun. Let's not go through all that again, please."

Ol' Jim was quiet for a long time—about 5.4 miles—and then he spoke: "Okay."

"What'd you say?" I asked.

"I said, 'Okay.' Okay—we'll not go through all that again. I'll try to be better."

Now I was the quiet one, feeling guilty.

It was a long way home. About the time we got to Food 4 Less, Jim finally broke the silence.

"Hey, John, it really looks like it's gonna be a dandy summer to travel!"

"Yeah, Jim. And thanks."

A Very Special Place

It was summertime in the early 1930s and life was grand. Getting to spend several weeks on the top of Magazine Mountain was a blessed relief from Conway's heat and humidity, though my older brother and I, then in our early elementary school years, were not particularly conscious of such things as summer heat. We just knew that heat and humidity were something about which adults complained, and that "mountain air" was a blessed relief. Our younger brother, just a baby, was too small to care either way about such things.

But most of all we knew that Magazine Mountain in the summer meant being free from school, taking long hikes in the woods, seeing snakes and occasional bobcats and perhaps even a bear. It was having grand family fun in our mountain cabin, getting to swim in the cold spring-fed pool, being chased by wild mountain cows and sleeping under the stars at night. It was listening to tall tales told by old, skinny, leathery mountaineers who smelled finely of green sawdust, Bull Durham and soured sweat.

It was a grand time indeed.

One of the highlights of such summers was when our father, who as pastor of Conway's First Methodist Church had to spend most of the week on the job, would come up to the mountain for a few days with his vacationing family.

On the day Dad was to arrive, Mother would pack a picnic lunch for my older brother and me and the two of us would hike down to the Big Tree, a very special place. There we would wait, not too patiently but with great anticipation, stopping our playing every few minutes or so to listen for Dad's car coming up the mountain.

There was something magic about that anticipation. The long, deep-rutted mountain road, with dozens of hairpin turns, was so steep that it caused even the stoutest vehicle to strain and groan as it made its way up what we proudly boasted was "the highest point between the Rockies and Alleghenies" (only to learn years later that some mountain in Oklahoma claimed that distinction).

After what was usually several hours, and after numerous false alerts, we finally would hear the first tell-tale sounds of our old family car huffing and puffing its way up the mountain road. Dad was coming!

The high point came when, at the last hairpin curve a half-mile or so down the road, our father would sound our "family signal" on the car horn—a series of three short and long blasts, "beep-beeeep, beep-beeeep, beep-beeeep!"

"He's coming! Dad's coming!"

Last week I stood by the side of my father's hospital bed, trying to choke back the knot in my throat as I watched this once stout, robust man talk as though life had been turned back a half-century. His once more-than-six-foot, 200-pound athletic frame now was reduced to a gaunt, skinny 140 pounds, eyes sunken and grip weakened, victim of a condition that robbed him, at least at times, of the present but graciously gave him the best gifts of the past.

"I think I hear them," he said. "I think I hear the cars coming up the mountain!" He smiled as if he knew more than his confusion indicated.

I told my mother—as much for my sake as for hers—that God is gracious, enabling us, when life almost wears out, to once again enjoy the grand good times of long ago.

There'll always be a Big Tree.

A Nice Thanksgiving

The first reports were on the radio as I pulled out of the Gazette parking lot Wednesday evening, headed for home.

The multicar pileup on the freeway sounded serious. A Med-Flight helicopter was on the ground and medical personnel were attending several injured persons. A child, the reporter was saying, had been severely hurt. One sensed that the reporter knew more than he was telling.

Thanksgiving Eve. I thought of the parting that co-workers shared as they left the office a few moments earlier: "Have a nice Thanksgiving."

A nice Thanksgiving.

A light rain was falling as I merged onto the freeway, headed in the opposite direction from the accident. Cars across the median were backing up, stopping. The frequent radio reports gave more grim details—at least two other multivehicle pileups had occurred in the same area.

A nice Thanksgiving.

It's a day later, now, Thanksgiving Day afternoon. We

know, now, that a little boy is dead. We know that others are suffering various degrees of injuries. We know that scores of lives have experienced loss and pain and are going through all those many difficulties that attend such tragic happenings.

And this was just one event, on one freeway, in one town, in one state, in one country.

Have a nice Thanksgiving.

I have, in fact, had a nice Thanksgiving Day, on the afternoon of which these thoughts are written. I've visited with and had turkey and pecan pie with no less than 27 assorted kinds of kinfolks, all in one house and all of whom behaved remarkably well, given the confinement. Someone said there'd have been 44 if all the others, God bless 'em, had been there.

Mercy.

It's been a nice Thanksgiving. But those freeway memories linger.

The thought came, that Thanksgiving Eve on the freeway: how much *at the mercy* of one another we all are! I was at the mercy of that fellow in the eighteen-wheeler I saw in my rear-view mirror, bearing down on my little car. And that lady in the vehicle in front of me, with the child in the safety seat, was at my mercy. Lives were in *my* hands. *My* life was in the hands of a bunch of other people.

I did have a nice Thanksgiving Day, and I'm grateful for it. But for a lot of people, Thanksgiving was not a nice day.

Do you suppose there can be comfort for those people, and for all the rest of us, in the thought that we're all in this together? Whether as individuals or nations, whether on freeways or at summit meetings, we're all at each other's mercy.

And not only are we at each other's mercy. We also *depend* on one another.

That fact, I submit, can bear a bit of thinkin'.

Again So Soon

It's refreshing, in this time of such rapid change and when we're surrounded by so much that's new and unknown, that we can be reminded of things that are old and familiar and don't change—like, for instance, ancient religious traditions and truths .... Thank God ... for such enduring occasions as our Palm Sundays and Holy Weeks and Easters and Passovers.

Gotcha

Merry Christmas!

Ah-ha! Gotcha!

We bet we're the first this year to wish you a Merry Christmas—except possibly for my neighborhood discount store, which seems to have had its Christmas stuff out since the Fourth of July.

But anyway, without another moment's delay you can start accumulating all that guilt and depression that, in this secularized society, have established themselves as inescapable ingredients in what should be one of the most joyful seasons of the year.

But why all this concern so early?

There's a reason: to alert you to a time-tested, guaranteed plan to make your religious holidays more meaningful. We wish this plan were our idea, but it isn't. And we wish telling you about this plan were also our idea, but that isn't the case, either. A letter from a friend 'splains what we're talking about.

"I need your help for one of my goals in life—namely, to have Christmas celebrated once again during Christmas instead of during Advent (or earlier) .... Christmas week has become such a letdown—partly because it no longer has any real meaning and partly because one is exhausted and used up from all the pre-Christmas parties and celebrations .... In most cases it is over after ten o'clock Christmas morning. What follows is one big letdown, spiritual and otherwise ....

"I don't think many people today know what the Epiphany is or what the Twelve Days of Christmas are. Help ...! I [want you] to write the column that will turn the world around .... I can hardly wait."

We, too.

My friend is right. Our secularized society has succeeded in siphoning the sustenance from the Season of

112

Seasons, leaving a sickening saccharinity to substitute for what should be a sublimely satisfying sojourn of the spirit.

Shame. Supershame.

As my friend notes, Advent, which begins four Sundays before Christmas, is not a time to "celebrate Christmas." It is, rather, a "getting ready" time. It's a time of quiet contemplation, a period of grand, mysterious anticipation. Advent quickens our spiritual senses, opens our minds to truths that shun busy days and prepares our hearts to receive a great good news.

Then, after proper preparation, Christmas may truly be celebrated on the day itself and, even more effectively, throughout the "Twelve Days of Christmas" until Epiphany, January 6. According to ancient tradition, Epiphany, associated variously with the visit of the Magi or the baptism of Jesus, marks "the full manifestation" of Christ as God Incarnate.

So there you have it. Christmas-lovers may take heart. There *are* ways to shake the shackles of suffocating secularism. There are ways to be set free to sail sublimely toward the sunrise of spiritual serenity. Those ways are called by some old names: Advent, Epiphany, Christmastide.

Now you know. So go ye and don't mess up again this year.

Advent Gives Us Angels

One might think that after a couple of thousand years Advent would lose its attraction. But it doesn't. The season, which symbolizes humanity's anticipation of the coming of a Savior, speaks to such basic human longings that it is assured immortality.

Advent, with all its hope, is here to stay.

One could wish there were something new to be said about the season. But on reflection it is enough to know that Advent's gifts—though always newly discoverable—are the old, time-honored, dependable, ever-needed gifts.

Consider those gifts. There is anticipation and encouragement and hope and renewal of spirit. A quick writing and casual reading of such words cannot adequately capture their profound meaning.

Advent calls for pondering.

Advent marries humanity's greatest needs with God's grandest gifts. Advent brings optimism to our discouragement, light to our darkness, joy to our sorrow, the promise of victory to our defeats.

To winter, Advent brings spring. To uncertainty it brings assurance. To lostness it brings foundness.

There is a little-noted dimension of Advent: its power. Advent's power it that of all great religious ideas—it is concerned with the grand, fundamental issues of the ages.

Advent knows our most profound yearnings. When we despair, Advent's ancient prophecies point to a Deliverer.

When the dark night of the soul closes in, Advent shows its star.

When the world's babble overwhelms us, Advent gives us angels, singing.

Advent tells of an exciting journey. It shows us wise men venturing from afar, kings and shepherds bringing gifts, children—and even animals—who know that some grand event is about to transpire.

Advent reminds us that God is always capable of surprising us. The season teases us, hinting that the grandest gifts may come in the most unexpected way. Advent regenerates feelings we thought belong only to children. It gives rebirth to the magic, the exhilaration of wonder.

Advent says to an anxious, frightened world that there is reason to hope. It tells us God wants to come, ever again, into creation.

We could do worse, these busy days before Christmas, than ponder the Advent message—that the Great Surpriser is poised again to shower us with unimaginable gifts.

Of Bombs and Babies

Even before the first phrase of that marvelous Advent hymn "Once in Royal David's City" had been sung by the Hendrix College Choir (with the stirring descant grandly sounded by the processing choir and accentuated by the pipe organ), the stage had been set for what was to follow: the annual lump-in-the-throat evening, that teary-eyed time when one is finally made fully aware that Advent has, in fact, come 'round once again and that Christmas in sure to happen soon.

Since our own college days at Hendrix, my wife and I, and later our children, have made the annual Candlelight Carol Service a part of our family Christmas tradition. Even now, although our four children are away from home—perhaps especially now—the event is a part of what the holidays are all about.

Like most family traditions, the occasion has a significance not easily expressed. It is one of those warm, quiet times when one finally can slow down amidst the haste of the season and ponder awhile.

At this particular concert, in Conway's First United Methodist Church, my wife and I enjoyed the music and spoken words while surrounded by friends of many years past in the sanctuary where I had joined the church and attended as a child.

The evening had been spent in the company of friends around a banquet table singing carols and hearing the never-old Christmas story once again.

And then the Candlelight Carol Service, recalling ancient prophecies and songs by angels and journeys of shepherds and stories of wise men bearing gifts—all to herald the birth of a baby.

The birth of a baby!

How strange—how utterly paradoxical, how naive—the ancient account seems in a modern-day setting. In a time when military might and geopolitical huckstering and economic clout seem the real power structures, the ancient declaration is made once again: that the Almighty Creator has ordained that it is through a *baby*, born in a cow shed and destined to be of the earth's poor and disfranchised, that the world is to be saved.

Preposterous!

As the young college students sang, bombs were bursting in Lebanon; covert wars were being fought in Central America; missiles were being placed in Europe; threats were being made to place Russian nuclear submarines off the coast of the United States; military alliances were being strengthened and arms sales extended and major increases in military budgets proposed. And over it all the shadow of a mushroom cloud was threatening to blot out all light, even Bethlehem's tiny star.

And there we sat, listening to songs about the birth of a baby.

Do babies really count for much in a world where human destiny hangs on the whims of the *real* power brokers? What could all these ancient prophecies and Bible stories and beautiful songs and quaint tales have to do with Lebanon and Nicaragua and Washington and Moscow and Afghanistan and Dublin?

The answer has something to do with what the Bible calls "the foolishness of God."

Our feeble efforts to expound on the mystery and wisdom of it all seem out of place—if not irreverent—on such Advent evenings. It is enough to sit and wonder. And marvel. And shed a few tears that, in spite of all reason to the contrary, reflect a deep, abiding joy.

Such occasions are a time to let the season, with its grand celebrations, work its eternal miracle once again: the renewal of hope and faith.

Let's Get This Over With

Okay, let's get this over with.

What we're talking about is all this annual agonizing over the Christmas blues. It's about time for this year's barrage of Christmas blues complaints to begin.

Christmas blues. So what else is new. We suspect the Wise Men from the East had the Christmas blues—as, probably, did the shepherds and maybe even the angels that sang those dandy first-Christmas songs.

Christmas blues? What about Joseph and Mary themselves? Ever try to get a room in Bethlehem at tax time? Ever been handed the kind of assignment given Mary and Joseph? We don't know the half of Christmas blues.

People—sensitive people, anyway—have always had times when they were depressed or overwhelmed with life. And it's totally understandable that holidays can be especially productive of such feelings. The reasons are obvious and have been analyzed *ad nauseum* and don't need any more encouragement from us.

Christmas blues happen. So let's get them over with and get on with the joy of the season.

Ah—the joy of the season! Let's hear it for the joy of the season.

The joy of the season. That's another thing that

happens every year about this time—at least to those folks who'll pause long enough to let it happen.

Real joy—not that shallow "happiness" that misguided people are always chasing—is the true Christmas miracle. Real joy is the realization—sometimes sudden, sometimes a slow-blooming awareness—that there's a wonder and beauty and grandness and marvelousness and excitement and splendidness about life that's more powerful than all the blues that either hard times or good times can foist on us.

Real joy is knowing there doesn't have to be "happiness" all the time, that life consists of more than an abundance of trinkets and continual "satisfaction." Real joy has to do with what the world might call strange associates—such things as work, wonder, mystery, faith, and, yes, even doubt. Real joy is a treasure hidden along steep, rocky paths—suffering, sorrow, even failure.

Real joy has to do with God's surprises—such as babies in mangers and strong men on crosses and empty tombs and sunrises.

Happiness is a harlot who sells cheap. Joy is a lover who stays the winter.

Advent is a time to prepare to receive the grand miracle and mystery of joy.

Scram, blues. Come on, joy!

Well Worth Celebrating

By this time, the packages have been opened, the Christmas stockings emptied and the living room is a mess. In spite of the current resistance to stereotypes, Mom is probably in the kitchen, Dad is in the easy chair, and the youngsters are trying to get someone to find a store that's open so they can buy batteries for all those batteries-not-included toys.

It's Christmas Day. It's that once-in-a-year, one-of-a-kind experience. Enjoy it, make the most of it, endure it, or do whatever you must with it. But most of all, sometime during the day make an effort to take in this day's special meanings of peace, love, joy, and hope.

These 24 hours won't come around again for another 365 days.

For multitudes of people, Christmas more than any other day evokes a splendid collage of emotions, meanings, and memories. It's a truly unique day, a time marked by the excitement of giving and receiving gifts, by family reunions, merriment, and joy. And, especially for the older ones among us, it's a time of recollection and reflection.

It was in the early 1930s, that Christmas in Fayetteville, when we stood on the city square outside the window of Campbell-Bell Dry Goods Store, watching that marvelous giant Lionel electric train make its oval journeys. Past little farmlands, across a bridge, through a tunnel, beside a little village—around and around again and again it would go. If only two little boys could ever have a train like that!

And then, on Christmas morning, to come into the living room at the Methodist parsonage and there, under the tree, to see the dream, the miracle, come true!

Christmas, our legends tell us, is for everyone.

For children, it is anticipation, excitement, a special wonder and magic that no other time of the year can match. Time cannot erase that magic.

For parents, it is that particular joy of enabling one's own children to have the same happy experiences of the season that they recall from their own childhood.

For grandparents and great-grandparents, it's that same joy multiplied twice, even three times, over.

It was snowing that mid-December day, now more than 20 years ago, as we made our annual trek into the woods to find a Christmas tree. The damp, swirling snow promised to add another several inches to the layer of white already covering the Ozark hills around Berryville.

For our three children, ranging in age from four to seven and bundled in heavy coats, scarves, and caps, it was tough, but delightful, going.

When "the right tree" was finally found, it was cut, dragged to the car, brought home, and placed in our living room from where its special fragrance would grace the entire house. A beautiful, living thing from deep in the forest, adding its silent secrets to the mysteries of the season.

We are frequently reminded these days that Christmas, for a not-insignificant number of people, is a time of depression. For such persons, the season cannot be over too soon. There's sadness in this—that the season associated with joy and peace should be a time of difficulty. Perhaps it would help, in some small way, if others could say they understand, they care.

Sometime during Christmas Day, there should be a quiet time, a time apart. A time when visiting and holiday activities can be put aside, and a period of solitude can be enjoyed. A time, simply, to think, to reflect on the special meanings of the day.

Quiet times on Christmas Day can bring tears—either of joy (especially of joy) or, if necessary, of sorrow. The day has a message for both occasions.

Christmas is one of two days—New Year's Day is the other—that are "watershed" days. They mark the end of the year's major holiday season and signal a return to normalcy. We go back to our regular schedules, shopping becomes routine, once again life falls back into place.

But "life as usual" is a misnomer for those who have

truly participated in Christmas. Such folk go back to their regular routines knowing that in spite of all bad news loose in the world today, there is a day that reminds us that love, peace, and hope are powerful realities in the world.

It's Christmas Day. Smile about it. Enjoy it. Cry a moment over it. But most of all, rejoice in it.

The First Saturday

Now that you've had a couple of days to get over the holidays, perhaps you're thinking it's time to get back to business.

But whoa, not so fast.

First, you've got to fulfill what is perhaps the most unsung of the season's rituals: the First Saturday of the New Year ritual.

Most of you, of course, are well acquainted with the ancient First Saturday ritual. For those of you who may have missed it, the observance is your absolutely last chance to do all those New Year-type things you meant to do on New Year's Day but either were too busy or forgot to do.

If putting things off is your style, First Saturdays were made for you.

First Saturdays offer you the absolutely final last chance to do your New Year's reflecting, meditating, planning, resolving, promising, and general pledging-to-do-better-this-year stuff. After the First Saturday is over, it's too late—the New Year is really here.

Now, if you took care of all your New Year's business already, or if you don't need any of this kind of thing, then you can forget this First Saturday ritual and get on with 1987. But for the rest of you, this is your absolutely last chance.

First, if you thought you could get by without making any New Year's resolutions but found that you couldn't, this is your opportunity. Oh yes, we know that the making of New Year's resolutions is old-fashioned and perhaps ineffective, probably creates guilt, and is most likely not too smart. But if done properly, the practice can be a constructive one.

Next comes the traditional First Saturday future-gazing time. This is when you sit a spell and contemplate the unknown, when you gaze, as it were, into the future. Do it now. The real New Year begins at midnight.

This brings us to the final element in the First Saturday ritual: being grateful. Be quiet for a time and practice the attitude of gratitude.

This brings us to the point of these ramblings: that whatever time of year it may be, gratitude is perhaps the most appropriate, most timely of all attitudes.

Gratitude wears well. Gratitude bears up with the times.

None of us knows what the New Year may hold. That mystery is part of the gift, part of the excitement.

Yes, L-E-N-T

Many people know it, many don't: today is Ash Wednesday.

Ash Wednesday?

That's the first day of Lent.

Yes, Lent. L-e-n-t. It's a religious season, a season in the Christian Year.

Most folk, of course, don't need that kind of elemental

introduction to the 40-day season (not counting Sundays) that immediately precedes Easter. For Lent is perhaps the best known of the major seasons of the Christian Year, though that distinction might go to Advent, which begins on the fourth Sunday before Christmas and opens the Christian Year.

Although strictly observed in the Roman Catholic, Orthodox, and the more liturgical or "high church" elements within Protestantism, the seasons of the Christian Year are not widely observed by what may be called the "new evangelical" and independent, nondenominational churches. But for the more traditional communions, the Christian Year has great significance.

What, then, about Ash Wednesday and Lent?

The term "ash" comes from an early Middle Ages custom in which ashes (in some traditions from burned palm leaves used in Palm Sunday services the previous year) are placed on the forehead of penitent worshipers and, in later practice, on the congregation generally.

The date of Ash Wednesday, and hence of Easter Day, varies annually. For non-Orthodox Western Christians, the date of Easter is set as the first Sunday following the first full moon after the Spring equinox. (Or, as stated in the *Episcopal Book of Common Prayer*, "Easter Day is always the first Sunday after the full moon that falls on or after March 21. It cannot occur before March 22 or after April 25.")

The word "Lent" comes from an Anglo-Saxon word meaning spring; thus the season has been associated with nature's pattern of reawakening, rebirth, and new life.

Lent has been associated with several highlights of Christian faith-history: it was originally 40 hours, rather than days, and commemorated the time between the crucifixion on Good Friday and the resurrection on Easter morning. It has been linked with the 40 days Moses spent on Mount Sinai, the 40 days of Jesus' temptation in the wilderness, and the 40 days between the resurrection and the ascension.

The Lenten season traditionally has been associated with fasting or other forms of self-denial. Early, it was observed as a period of preparation for baptism at Easter.

But it is by focusing on Jesus' pain, rejection, and ultimate crucifixion, that Lent—especially in its Passion Sunday and Good Friday services—makes its unique contribution of highlighting a central theme in the gospel: the fact of suffering, its meaning, and its redemptive uses.

Whatever its historical associations, Lent's "practical" significance is seen as an opportunity for the church and the faithful to prepare for the Easter event. Easter, with its triumphant message of victory over death, does not belong in Lent. It is the beginning of Eastertide, a season when the resurrection's messages of hope and faith are emphasized.

Lent invites reflection. The season comes to our modern world almost as a stranger. To many, it comes as an intruder. For in the midst of the world's noise, Lent calls the faithful to silence.

Lent confronts an affluence-seeking society with the demanding claims of sacrifice. It has the effrontery to suggest to a self-serving age that salvation is to be found in self-denial, in service to others.

To a culture saturated with the trappings of superficial success, Lent speaks of self-giving. It elevates the sacrificial spirit. In a society that shuns pain, Lent suggests there is redemption to be found through suffering. It mystifies us with the magnificent defeat that is the cross.

To our emphasis on freedom and liberty, Lent speaks of discipline, duty, and discipleship. In the midst of multiplied activities, the season calls the devout to quietness and meditation.

Lent comes as a stranger. A passing stranger. If we would entertain Lent as a guest, we must do so on its own terms, not ours. If we only indulge this eccentric, impertinent visitor, we miss its message and lose its gifts.

Lent offers the possibility of "coming to consciousness" for the human spirit. It is a 40-day journey of the soul, a priority pilgrimage for the devout.

Along Comes Religion

Just about the time we've shaken off December's Advent and Hanukkah celebrations and thought it safe to get back to business as usual, along come a couple of other religious observances to disturb our secular tranquility. This time it's Lent and Passover.

That's the trouble with religion—it's always poking its nose in our business.

Lent, which begins Ash Wednesday, includes the 40 weekdays before Easter. Observed since the fourth century, the season is a time when Christians contemplate the life, message, and sacrificial suffering of Jesus. The season traditionally has been marked by confession and penitence, though such heavy themes have been tempered by the knowledge that the splendor of Easter's message lies close at hand.

Passover is a time when both Jews and Christians commemorate the exodus of Jews from Egypt. The annual observance, based on events recorded in the twelfth chapter of Exodus, celebrates the grand, universal themes of liberation, freedom, and hope.

In addition to the obvious benefits the faithful receive from these two ancient observances, the two celebrations have a tremendous capacity to disturb. Both Lent and Passover possess the quality inherent in all authentic biblical religion—that it comforts the afflicted and afflicts the comfortable.

When faithfully observed, Lent and Passover come as intrusions into our satisfied lives. To a comfortable and complacent church or synagogue, the respective observances come as an affront, an impertinence. To a secularized world consumed by self-interest and the lust for power, to a world that too often runs roughshod over the most basic human values, Lent and Passover come as an ancient judgment.

Serious observers of Lent, examining afresh the life and message of Jesus, are confronted with a fact too easily forgotten by the church—that these are radical teachings indeed; that this Jesus was, in fact, a dangerous man, a threat to religion as usual, an upsetter of the status quo. This is a man who bids us love our enemies, judge ourselves before judging others, forgive wrongdoers, share our possessions, put others before ourselves. Such admonitions, when taken seriously, have the capacity to turn the world upside down.

Serious observers of Passover are reminded that liberation, freedom, and hope are not just abstract themes, not just rhetoric for preachers and politicians. Passover challenges the faithful to put up or shut up regarding their boast of being champions of social justice.

Passover takes a congregation out of the security of a stained-glass sanctuary and hurls it into the risky, often unlovely secular world. It confronts the faithful with the plight of people unjustly imprisoned by oppressive governments, those suppressed by racial and sexual discrimination, those rendered powerless by greedy and unjust rulers and social structures.

Lent and Passover are religious observances that nourish the human spirit. They also speak of enduring values by which the larger society is both guided and judged.

We could do worse than ponder awhile the profound meanings of these ancient observances.

Again So Soon

It's almost Holy Week again. Tomorrow's Palm Sunday. Soon comes Maundy Thursday and then Good Friday. Before you know it, Easter Sunday itself will be upon us once again.

But we went through all this just a year ago. You mean we've got to do it again? So soon?

Yep. And again next year. And the year after that. And the year after that and so on for the duration, as they say.

But this presents problems for those of us who are expected to say something new and brilliant each twelve months about these seasons that just keep repeating themselves year after year. You'd think that if we got it right, just once, we could skip a few years.

But it doesn't work out that way, you say.

Okay. It's just as well, we suppose.

But can anything new be said about all this Holy Week business?

Probably not. And in that fact, we submit, lurks some good news.

It's refreshing, in this time of such rapid change and when we're surrounded by so much that's new and unknown, that we can be reminded of things that are old and familiar and don't change—like, for instance, ancient religious traditions and truths. We need the security that such dependability and stability affords. Thank God, we say, for such enduring occasions as our Palm Sundays and Holy Weeks and Easters and Passovers.

But about the time we settle in with such religion-as-usual attitudes, we become aware that something's not quite right about our contentment. It occurs to us, as we contemplate the Palm Sunday events, that this Jesus we honor was involved in some very dangerous, risky business. No easy religion-as-usual here. Jesus was on the move, nearing the end of a very perilous journey. Jesus was bound for Jerusalem, determined to keep a rendezvous with a cross. A crown of thorns, a spear in the side, death and a tomb were his destination.

Not much comfort there, neither for this Jesus nor for us, his ease-seeking twentieth-century fans.

Maybe Maundy Thursday, then.

Not much partying there, either. We see a rather somber bunch, preoccupied with dismal themes.

And Good Friday?

Forget it—unless your idea of fun includes a cross and a slow agonizing death.

We're left with some pretty unfun themes—themes that our success-oriented, materialism-centered, personal-gratification-styled "Christianity" has trouble with.

Perhaps it is well, after all, that Holy Week with its somber themes of suffering and sacrifice comes 'round regularly every year.

We suspect that most of us, constantly bombarded with a cheapgrace Christianity, may look back on Holy Week's annual heavy reminders and say, with honesty, thanks—we needed that.

Almost Too Much

Easter is almost too much for us, too grand for us. It is one of those occasions for which cold words, alone, are inadequate. To tell Easter's story requires the fullness of our art—our song, our dance, our drama, our hot language of poetry.

Easter is not so much an event as it is an experience. We do Easter no favor when we insist that it be taken too literally, thus restricting its meaning and message to the limits of our understanding. Easter is impatient with our literalisms.

Easter is a mystery, a grand mystery whose glories may be marveled at and admired and stood in awe of but never fully understood.

As love and beauty and truth do not reveal their essence to safe verbal inquiry, so is Easter a grand life-principle that yields her secrets only to those dreamers and adventurers who are willing to risk the leap of faith.

Easter is God's grand "Yes!" to His experiment. It is life's great shout of victory. By taking the sting and victory from death, the symbol of life's final defeat, Easter brings the supreme gift: hope.

Easter is the perfect gift for the person who has everything—or nothing.

Easter is our comforter. It takes us, with our keenest sorrows—whether of death or some other vast pain—and it nurtures us. Easter takes our most profound fears—whether of nuclear holocaust or the spoiling of the earth or the loss of our corporate sanity—and it bolsters us with hope.

Easter is our teacher, prodding and reminding us that the Creator's aim is life, not death. Easter begs us cease our foolish ways that threaten His dreams for us.

Easter is our mother, nestling us tenderly in her arms, humming to us her lovely spring melodies and whispering that all is well, that we need not be afraid.

Easter is almost too grand for us. Almost—but not quite.

It is enough.

Of Hummingbirds and Children

*The gospel [makes] prophetic judgments on political op-
pression, social injustice, economic disparity, violence ....
The mandate of the gospel qualifies the church to speak its
mind on the issues at hand.*

Of Tides and Times

William Shakespeare said it: "There is a tide in the affairs of men, which, taken at the flood, leads on to fortune; omitted, all the voyage of their life is bound in shallows and in miseries."

Most of us know something about that. A few have tasted the fortune; more have suffered the miseries.

But whatever, Shakespeare's wisdom remains. The Bible confirms it: there's such a thing as the fullness of time.

We boldly suggest that nothing less than that is happening right now in these pre-summit meeting days when the world's two great superpowers are flirting with each other, however rudely. Could it be—just could it be—that right now we're poised on a "fullness of time" moment in regard to that most elusive of all goals, world peace?

It excites and gladdens the heart to think so. It boggles the mind to imagine it. It quickens the spirit to yearn for it. And it saddens the heart, and frightens it, to know that such a moment is so precarious, so constantly in danger of being lost.

Let us pray for the peace of Jerusalem.

And of Moscow. And Washington. And Little Rock and Adelaide and New Delhi and Beijing and Murmansk and Managua and Yokohama and Blue Eye and all the unknown hamlets of the planet and all the earth's people.

And after prayers, what?

Sermons abound in response to that question, so surely one more won't hurt.

■We can work on that primary evil that keeps the likelihood of war alive: suspicion, mistrust, and ignorance of other people—notably for us in this instance "the Russians."

■We can rid ourselves of outdated trust in weapons to ensure security, and of our age-old maintenance of an "enemy" (currently "the Communists") to keep alive those hatreds thought necessary to preserve nationalism and power.

■We can work for justice, that condition necessary to any lasting peace. We can examine what it means to be the privileged among the powerless.

■We could, even, repent of our sin, with all the attendant changing that such a radical act entails.

For people of faith, the fullness of time is always a possibility. So, too, in this nuclear age, is the possibility that our mutual enmity will write "finish" to the human experiment, triggering the final ebb tide in the sometimes glorious, sometimes tragic affairs of man.

Just as heaven should be stormed with prayers for peace, so our world leaders should be put on notice, rudely if necessary:

We *demand* that this fullness-of-time moment not be lost! We *demand* that you agree together to begin putting away these horrible weapons that otherwise will bury us all! In the name of all living beings and all who yet may live, we *demand* peace!

Pastors and Prophets

Once again some of Arkansas's principal religious leaders have demonstrated that they aren't willing to let it pass when the community's ethical and moral sensibilities have been affronted. On Wednesday, six top officials of Christian and Jewish groups called a press conference to express their concern about the "undue emphasis" given capital punishment during the recent primary election campaigns, particularly by candidates in the gubernatorial races.

The candidates, the religious leaders said, gave the appearance of trying to outdo each other in a push toward executing someone. The clergy called on candidates in the primary runoff and general election campaigns "to reassess the amount of emphasis they place on capital punishment," to "address topics that more directly affect Arkansans" (they mentioned education, economics, and employment), and to "be concerned about the total integrity of their political campaigning."

The group included the bishops of the Episcopal, Roman Catholic, and United Methodist churches in Arkansas, the rabbi of the largest Reform synagogue in the state, and the principal executives of the Christian Church (Disciples of Christ) and Presbyterian churches in Arkansas.

The religious leaders spoke to an issue that has needed such a public airing: that politicians have "used" such issues as crime and capital punishment to play to the crowd, and that in doing so have both compromised themselves and, by appealing to humanity's worst instincts, insulted the electorate.

The way to get votes, the reasoning is, is to get tough on crime and criminals. Not the least of the objections to such an approach is that it placates the voters and gets the candidates off the hook, relieving them of making constructive suggestions on how to handle such complex criminal justice issues as restitution, punishment and rehabilitation.

The clergymen stated their belief that capital punishment "is incompatible with the basic principles of the Judeo-Christian faith" and that "the power to kill remains in conflict with all [the state's] other responsibilities and aims." The state's chief goals, they said, are "strengthening, affirming, and prolonging life."

The clergymen insisted that their statement not be interpreted as a glossing over of the knotty problems related to criminal justice. "We're not anxious to let [hardened criminals] loose on the streets," one said.

Their point, another said, is that capital punishment should be seen "as part of the abundance of violent and volatile acts with which contemporary society is obsessed." By approving capital punishment, he said, "we all participate in that violence. Our hands are on the switch .... There's no holy way to kill another human being."

This is far from being the first time that Arkansas's principal religious leaders have spoken out on current issues that have both political and moral dimensions. Though each of these leaders would insist on speaking for himself on such issues, several of them were among groups which, during the past few years, have made public statements on such issues as the effects of high utility rates and grocery prices to the poor, threats to good race relationships, dangers to public education, the effects of President Reagan's cuts in human services, and the dangers of a nuclear arms race.

If centuries of Judeo-Christian tradition have taught us anything, it is that when a community's chief pastors take such prophetic stances, that community is well served.

Of Hummingbirds and Children

I'd rather think about those lovely little hummingbirds that grace our patio throughout the day, darting in to take a quick, though sometimes lingering, drink of nectar from the feeder that hangs just a few feet from where we sit each evening to help the day do its endings.

Lovely little creatures, each a work of majesty, each a miracle.

And I'd rather think of that little squirrel I surprised the other morning at the edge of our porch, digging up a pecan he had hidden last fall.

And, of course, there are our grandchildren, ages seven and five, wonderful subjects for thought any time of the day. Just a couple of weeks ago Grandmother and I helped them and their parents move to Oklahoma, so they've been especially on our minds of late.

This would be a good weekend to think of such things. But such thoughts will be difficult to sustain because there's going to be lots of news about things totally foreign to hummingbirds and squirrels and grandchildren.

This weekend marks the 40th anniversary of the bombing of Hiroshima and Nagasaki. It was four decades ago this week that the horrors of nuclear weapons were unleashed on this lovely and fragile planet.

Though Monday morning quarterbacking isn't worth much, we personally have never been convinced it was "necessary" for our side to use the atomic bomb. Whatever may have been gained in bringing the war in the Pacific to a quicker conclusion—and there is much evidence that challenges that theory—our distinction of being the first nation to use nuclear weapons is an indictment that will remain throughout history. However long time lasts, this peace-loving land will be remembered as "first to have used the bomb."

This weekend there will be an estimated 100,000 persons, mostly women, in Washington to "wrap" the Pentagon, the Capitol, and the Lincoln Memorial with peace ribbons. The demonstration, a gentle one, reflects a growing yearning for peace felt throughout the earth, a groundswelling wave of good news in a good-news-hungry world.

For months, in communities across this country, women and children and men have made small banners depicting "things they would not want to see perish" in a nuclear war.

In a response that can only be called astounding, an estimated dozen miles of such banners have been sewn or painted or drawn or woven, a glorious outpouring, a veritable crescendo of shouts and prayers for peace from hamlets and farms and cities and villages throughout this land.

Add to the list of things held dear, my hummingbirds and my squirrels and my grandchildren.

Of Popes and Presidents

The scene has become increasingly familiar in recent years. The pope descends the steps of a jetliner, is greeted by heads of state and church dignitaries, moves through teeming throngs and reaches out to the sea of hands extended from the sometimes jubilant, sometimes weeping crowds.

Such happenings were viewed around the world again this week. This time it was Central America, where Pope John Paul II, the most traveled pontiff in history, visited five countries in what was repeatedly referred to as an embattled region. It was, one account stated, the pope's most dangerous trip to date. Threats against his life were reported on at least two occasions.

If this was Pope John's most dangerous journey, it was also one of his most timely and relevant ones. And it revealed, in sometimes dramatic fashion, the paradoxical nature of Christian responsibility: pastoral care and prophetic admonition.

"One should be with those who suffer," the pope said to reporters who asked why he would make such a dangerous trip. "I speak of peace, concord, and hope," he said at his initial stop in Costa Rica.

But later, especially in Nicaragua, El Salvador, and

Haiti, the pontiff had occasion, in several truly startling confrontations, to thunder the gospel's prophetic judgments on political oppression, social injustice, economic disparity, violence, and the various other exploitations that combine to subject the region to continued conflict and suffering.

There was a painful irony related to the pope's visit. On the eve of his vigorous call for a peaceful solution to Central America's violent conflicts, two presidents—Ronald Reagan in Washington and José Efrain Rios Montt in Guatemala—took actions that were at best an embarrassment and at worst an affront.

Mr. Reagan announced his intention to seek a minimum of $60 million in additional military aid to El Salvador and to increase by perhaps as many as three times the number of United States military advisers to that country. And General Montt refused to stay the execution, out of deference to the pope's visit, of six suspected terrorists.

It can be expected at such times to hear critics say the church "should not interfere in political issues," that politicians and military people know more than priests and religious leaders do about such things. But the fact is that the church, both Catholic and Protestant, has been more closely in touch with the harsh realities of the Central American situation and with the internal causes of the region's turmoil than has the Montt government or the Reagan administration.

That closeness, as well as the mandate of the gospel, qualifies the church to speak its mind on the issues at hand.

The visit by the leader of the world's 700 million Catholics points vividly to what some have only lately come to recognize: that the Roman Catholic Church is exerting a renewed and tremendously powerful influence internationally on major peace issues.

Another evidence of that influence is the American bishops' pastoral letter on peace, the third and perhaps final draft of which is due later this year. Similar statements by Catholic bishops in other countries, as well as by Protestant, Jewish, and other religious leaders, reflect the growing participation of religious groups in such matters.

Such statements, along with Pope John Paul's visits, remind the world of the way of peace. A post-Vietnam generation should know only too well the futility and consequences of attempts at military solutions to basically human problems.

The Apostle Paul, in the prelude to his magnificent discourse recorded in Chapter 13 of First Corinthians, has a word for the moment: "Behold, I show you a more excellent way."

"Going Bail" for Justice

It was a simple remark, made almost in passing, but it was profound. It was the kind of thing one would like to have thought of oneself.

Rev. William Sloane Coffin, Jr., said it. It came in a reply to a question posed in a recent interview when the prominent antiwar and civil rights activist, former Yale University chaplain, and current minister of Riverside Church at New York was at Little Rock to speak in the Ecumenical Lecture Series.

The question had to do with what should be the response of this country's religious community in the wake of Reagan administration budget cuts in social services and other human welfare programs. Dr. Coffin's response was quick: in the first place, he said, the amount required to pick up the slack from such cuts is far greater than could be met by the churches and synagogues. There's no way that religious groups could pick up such a tab, he said.

Then came the zinger: "And besides, charity should not go bail for justice."

The comment—a sleeper—merits prolonged, careful reflection: *Charity should not go bail for justice.*

The statement offers insight into what we suggest is one of society's most fundamental social and moral problems: we too often let injustice off the hook by throwing a few good works in its direction. By doing our quota of socially acceptable good deeds, we excuse ourselves from the larger responsibility to "do right."

■We give Christmas baskets because it makes us feel good and is a lot easier than the long, hard work required to overcome the wrongs that breed poverty. Charity goes bail for justice.

■We hire a few token minorities and yet fail to make those fundamental changes in our individual attitudes and social and economic structures that are necessary if humanity's age-old enemy, racism, is to be overcome. Charity goes bail for justice.

■We tell women they've come a long way, baby, and assure them that things are getting better, honey, and yet continue those practices that solidify male domination of society. Charity goes bail for justice.

■We fight a few battles for the oppressed but consistently reinforce systems that insure that the powerful get more power, the rich get richer and the oppressed become more oppressed. Charity goes bail for justice.

■We give our tithes and offerings, enabling good works to be done, and yet remain in willing bondage to corporate structures that frequently are the chief enemies of those we   purport to help. Charity goes bail for justice.

Harsh criticism, of course—and perhaps unfair to those who are working hard to overcome such wrongs. But the point is a legitimate one: charity too frequently enables us to avoid the larger responsibilities to be fair and just.

Charity is a noble, valued, and needed virtue. It is a

vital human quality, not to be disparaged. What is to be condemned, however, is society's willingness to let a little bit of charity take the place of the required measure of justice.

On the ultimate scales, justice weighs more than charity. We won't easily be let off the hook.

Tuesday and Wednesday

Tuesday and Wednesday the leaders of the world's two most powerful nations will sit down together in Geneva, Switzerland, to talk of peace. Two men. Two nations. One world. One destiny.

Some may think too much is being made of the occasion. We submit the opposite is true—that not enough *could* be made of the moment when two nuclear giants, the fate of the planet in their hands, come eyeball to eyeball.

That grand old maple tree on Caldwell Street in Conway is outdoing itself again this fall, blessing heart and soul with its splendid symphony of colors. Were mere leaves ever more radiant? Did sunlight and haze ever reveal such fire?

It is foolish, of course, to believe that what two men may do on a Tuesday and Wednesday could assure lasting peace among nations. It is equally foolish, as well as a distortion of faith, to believe that some divine power will save us in spite of our own willful madness in persisting to build larger arsenals of planet-destroying nuclear weapons.

Even the gods cannot save those bent on self-destruction. But even if God could save us in spite of ourselves, it is questionable, in light of our behavior that could destroy the planet, whether we are worthy of such a salvation.

But human beings must try. And even though the world most likely will go on after whatever is or isn't achieved next week in Geneva, the summit meeting is an all-too-rare opportunity in this planet's quest for peace.

The happy memory comes, the slow-motion recollection of grandchildren lost in innocent abandon that afternoon last summer, playing in our back yard. No particular occasion, this—except that every occasion of childhood joy is a golden moment, an open window through which one is granted a glimpse of the grandest gems of the realm.

One wonders—do Russians have grandchildren?

Come Tuesday and Wednesday, Mr. Reagan and Mr. Gorbachev will not be alone in their quest for peace. They will be surrounded, supported, "lifted up" by a host of unseen bit-players in this cosmic drama—individuals and groups throughout the world who will be praying for the success of the talks.

Autumn leaves fall and grand old trees make ready for whatever winter may bring, already preparing tiny buds for next spring's beginnings.

The world's children, happily weary with play, fall asleep and dream of tomorrow.

"You Can't Fool Us ..."

Somebody once said humanity's biggest problem is that there's always somebody eager to tell us what is humanity's biggest problem.

Religion, or at least some of religion's spokesmen, could rightly be accused of being, at times, that somebody. Some preachers and religious zealots seem eternally ready to announce what's wrong with us—and quick to volunteer advice on how we can go about correcting those wrongs.

To be on the receiving end of such unsolicited counsel can be unpleasant, irritating, and boring. But in spite of those prospects, it remains that there just might be a lot of truth in what some of those sometimes uncouth sons and daughters of Amos and Deborah and John and Paul are saying.

There *are* false prophets, to be sure, just as there are false doctors, lawyers, plumbers, journalists, mechanics, educators, and whatever. But in regard to the preachers, there's an old Book, upon which their whole case is based, that has proved reliable throughout the centuries. And that old Book makes some amazingly up-to-date observations concerning what's wrong with us.

For one thing, it tells us that we usually fight the wrong enemies. Whereas we choose to think in terms of other persons or countries as being the enemy, this Book speaks, rather, of "principalities and powers." It talks about such things as pride and greed and covetousness. It suggests that we look first at ourselves; that we get the log out of our own eye before we offer to remove the splinter from our neighbor's eye. It says the word—sin.

This Book talks about poverty and hunger as being enemies. It cites our failure to be good stewards of all creation. It is harsh in its judgment of our reluctance to be good brothers and sisters to one another. It talks about forgiving those who do wrong to us. It calls us to be peacemakers.

This Book also tells us that we seek our security in wrong places. It says that those who trust in chariots are fools, that the war horse is a vain hope for victory, that a king is not saved by his great army and that a warrior is not delivered by his great strength.

We are told, rather, that our security lies in something called "looking to the Holy One of Israel."

We're smarter than that, or course. We know that our real enemies are the Russians, the Communists. We know that we are supposed to consume the earth rather than conserve it for future generations. We know that it's not becoming for strong men to forgive one another. We know that it's sissy to be peacemakers. And we know that our real security lies in neutron bombs and MX missiles and B-1 bombers.

You can't fool us. What do we need with an old Book?

Hand-Holding Thoughts

Come 2:00 p.m. Sunday, we plan to be with a bunch of folks from the church we attend who will join an estimated 250,000 or more other Arkansans in clasping hands, symbolically if not actually, with millions of Americans in a coast-to-coast chain to raise money for this country's hungry and homeless.

Whatever else may be said of the Hands Across America event, it's a noble idea, worthy of encouragement and support.

But before a single hand is touched, let us get something off our chest. Be patient and squirm with us for a moment. It isn't easy to be the professional adversary and skeptic, but such folks are a necessary nuisance in a healthy democracy.

We fully expect, while standing in line, to have our cup filled with good feelings. We expect to be reaffirmed in our belief that this country does, in fact, contain a lot of good-hearted people who want to do right, who want to help their neighbors, who love justice and want to pursue righteousness.

But there are other thoughts we'll take to the line. At their core will be the comment of a preacher, a Yankee preacher at that, whose words of some five years ago still gnaw at our soul: "Our problem in this country is that we let charity go bail for justice."

144

Ponder that while standing in the sun.

To what extent do we Americans allow our good works to "go bail" for justice? To what extent do we let ourselves off the hook by doing good instead of doing right?

The point regarding hunger in this country is this: to what extent do our charitable reactions, as commendable as they may be, reinforce the unjust laws and social systems that help trap 35 million Americans in poverty and hunger today? Why does this country have the highest rate of poverty since 1965? Why, in 1985 alone, was poverty this country's greatest killer of children?

Are we somehow allowing our charity to go bail for justice?

Our nation is suffering a serious case of misplaced priorities. Most notable is our compulsion to seek security in militarism. All sorts of injustice come from that misplaced priority. Militarism may rightly be called a major cause of poverty.

The boast by Americans that "We're Number One!" among the world's nations in military might conceals some frightening realities: that we're seventh in life expectancy, thirteenth in infant mortality, tenth in student-teacher ratio, and twentieth in doctor-patient ratio. This is national security?

Is it a misplaced priority that one-third of this nation's scientists and engineers are under military contract?

While America is holding hands tomorrow to raise a paltry $25 million or so to feed and house the poor, our administration talks of annual requests of $4.8 *billion* for Star Wars, $4.2 billion for the MX "Peacekeeper," $100 million to buy guns for the terroristic "contras," those U.S.-backed counter-revolutionaries who are fighting the popularly elected government of Nicaragua, which just happens to be a sovereign nation with whom our country has diplomatic relations.

Hand-holders, don't let anybody con you into selling justice for a mess of charity. Don't let the poverty-bringers off with a wink—or a handclasp.

"Free Zone" Number Two

After a unanimous vote of one, which came during a remarkably peaceful caucus, my six-by-eight foot cubicle on the second floor of the Gazette Building has just been declared a Nuclear-Free Zone.

If my information is correct, we can boast being second only to the Unitarian Universalists out on Reservoir Road as having made such a public declaration locally. We're not ashamed to be number two.

The Unitarian brothers and sisters even went a step further: they published abroad their support of a mutual freeze on nuclear weapons and declared their opposition to the continuing arms race. Hear! Hear!

Furthermore, one Unitarian sister challenged other area religious groups to follow suit.

Let's hear it for the Unitarians!

A small thing, some might say. But nevertheless an important thing in a world that too long has tolerated an encroaching militarism that now threatens to write *finis* to the whole human experiment.

The sad fact is that this world is experiencing an epidemic of militarism that is fueling an arms race that now threatens to invade outer space. How ironic that "heaven" itself should become the deadly playground for madmen whose games can end only in the destruction of God's creation.

God knows, we've become a war-oriented world. Problems in Central America? Send a bunch of fighting ships to the Caribbean, conduct an illegal covert war in Nicaragua, build some permanent military bases in Honduras (contrary to United States law), send 5,000 troops to the area and let them flex their muscles for a half-year or more.

Trouble in Lebanon? Send in the troops. Put 30 United States warships off the coast.

Need "friends" throughout the world? Sell weapons to whoever can pay the price and to some who can't.

Similar or worse scenarios could be attributed to the other world powers, of course. But we must answer for ourselves.

Who's to blame for such a circumstance? Who are the villains?

It's easy to pounce on "the government." But don't overlook daddies and mommies who buy toy pistols for their children. And the writers of television scripts who glorify violence. And churches that are sleepy and content to wink at the continuous undermining of a country's morality.

And don't overlook an entrenched military machine. And an economic system enslaved to a war economy. And don't forget a mindset that seeks simplistic solutions, that throws bombs and dollars rather than logic and innovative reasoning at complex problems.

Perhaps the Unitarians are correct: begin at home. Start with your own ground.

Any other takers?

Only Dead Men

Mark Twain wrote it, but friends warned that it was too potent, too abrasive, that it would be considered an affront, a sacrilege. They advised that if it were printed at all, it should only be after the writer's death.

Reluctantly, Twain agreed. "I have told the truth," he said, "and only dead men can tell the truth in this world. It can be published after I am dead."

What was considered so radical, so dangerous?

It was a prayer. Twain wrote it in 1905 and called it "The War Prayer."

One Sunday morning, on the eve of a great battle, a minister prayed that God would bless the young soldiers in the congregation before they departed for the battlefield. The preacher asked God to "help them to crush the foe."

After the prayer a robed stranger entered the church, approached the pulpit and motioned for the preacher to stand aside. In an authoritative voice he told the startled congregation that the preacher had offered not one prayer, but two—one spoken, the other not. God had heard both, the stranger said, and added that he wanted to be sure the congregation knew the full import of what the preacher was asking.

To that end, the stranger said, he was commissioned by God to put the unspoken prayer into words:

"O Lord our Father, our young patriots, idols of our hearts, go forth to battle—be Thou near them!

"O Lord our God, help us to tear their soldiers to bloody shreds with our shells. Help us to cover their smiling fields with the pale forms of their patriot dead. Help us to drown the thunder of the guns with the shrieks of their wounded, writhing in pain. Help us to lay waste their humble homes with a hurricane of fire. Help us to wring the hearts of their unoffending widows with unavailing grief.

"Help us to turn them out roofless with their little children to wander unfriended the wastes of their desolated land in rags and hunger and thirst, sports of the sun flames of summer and the icy winds of winter, broken in spirit, worn with travail, imploring Thee for the refuge of the grave and denied it.

"For our sakes who adore Thee, Lord, blast their hopes, blight their lives, protect their bitter pilgrimage, make heavy their steps, water their way with their tears, stain the white snow with the blood of their wounded feet!

"We ask it, in the spirit of love, of Him who is the Source of Love. Amen."

Mark Twain, a dead man, told the truth about war.

In this time when so many leaders give lip service to peace while preparing for what could be the planet's last conflict, only live men and women can tell the horrible, unimaginable truth about war.

Time is too short for this world to wait for dead men to be its only prophets of peace.

Some Post-Fourth Reflections

I may be excused, perhaps, for marking the Fourth of July with something more than average interest. I happen to share the same birthday with my country—a matter, for me, of appropriate humility mixed with not-too-subtle pride.

(I can make the observation about the date of my birth that someone once made about the place of theirs: I was born on the Fourth of July because I wanted to be near my mother and she happened to be in the hospital delivery room on that particular morning.)

Pardon these other quick credentials to establish my

patriotism: when I greeted the world on the Independence Day morning I came complete with red hair, white skin and blue eyes and was given the middle name "Sparks," only incidentally a family name.

So, on the morning of the Fourth, when this is being written, it seems fitting to think patriotic thoughts.

It would be difficult to do otherwise, as my 40-minute drive to work was accompanied by a marvelous concert of John Philip Sousa marches, an appropriate encore to what I had seen earlier on television while eating my birthday breakfast of Country Morning cereal with sliced banana: the United States Marines Drum and Bugle Corps, followed by the Marines' "silent drill."

It was a stimulating morning—Sousa's marches leading my freeway foray through the marvelously crisp early morning air, gliding through the emerald green fields bordered by the skies flecked with white clouds dotted by graceful eagle-like birds faithfully about their morning chores. A natural setting for patriotic thinking.

What kept coming to mind, however, were individuals and events that all week had challenged our traditional understandings of patriotism. There were those two Arkansans, Paul Jacobs of North Little Rock and Duncan Bassett Murphy of Sulphur Springs, who had the impertinence to disturb my holiday celebrations by suggesting that patriotism may be expressed in some very untraditional—and to some, very unacceptable—ways.

Jacobs, convicted of failing to register for the draft and sentenced to prison, had forced us to consider an unpopular proposition—that it is patriotic to be willing to suffer for the conviction that freedom includes the right to speak out against a system that could force a young man to fight in a war his conscience may tell him is unjust.

And there was Murphy, the 65-year-old tree trimmer and long-time peace activist who had vowed to fast until his death unless the United States ceases its support of what he considers terrorism in Nicaragua.

I submit that these two individuals are giving us examples of "true" patriotism—not only legitimate American patriotism but a higher patriotism that may not be ignored by United States citizens who profess the universal biblical religions.

Another bit of music, a hymn, kept coming to mind on this morning of the Fourth of July:

This is my song, O God of all the nations,
A song of peace for lands afar and mine.
This is my home, the country where my heart is—
Here are my hopes, my dreams, my holy shrine.
But other hearts in other lands are beating
With hopes and dreams as true and high as mine.

My country's skies are bluer than the ocean,
And sunlight beams on clover leaf and pine.
But other lands have sunlight too, and clover,
And skies are everywhere as blue as mine.
Oh hear my song, thou God of all the nations,
A song of peace for their land and for mine.

Anchors in the Storm

The good news is that ... many and varied expressions of hope are being "lived out" daily around us. They give us quiet assurance and joy. They remind us that for people of the biblical faiths, hope and optimism are not options. They are responsibilities.

"Some Jesus Stories"

Most families have their own collection of family stories, tales based on happenings that through the years have become a part of their heritage. Even though such stories may be embellished, revised, or told in differing ways, they nevertheless remain a vital part of the family's identity. They are part of its own larger "faith story." One such tale from my own experience has come to mind on numerous occasions and may perhaps be used here to help make a point.

One summer about 50 years ago, when I was about five years old and my brother was seven and our youngest brother was yet to be born, we were on Mount Magazine, in Logan County, where our family frequently spent summer vacations. In those years it wasn't unusual to catch glimpses, or at least see evidence, of the numerous brown bears, wildcats, mountain lions, and even panthers that made their home among the mountain's rugged and remote bluffs.

One evening, in the company of friends, neighbors who formed a small summer community on the mountain, we were returning from a hike to the edge of fabled Bear Hollow. (The name itself, to a five-year-old, wasn't designed to inspire feelings of security. We recalled evenings in front of the fireplace, listening to oldtimers weave yarns about the wild animals of Bear Hollow.)

As we made our way along the narrow trail, suddenly a large animal—we never knew whether it was a bear or a mountain lion or whatever—frightened our dog and sent him yelping into the woods. The unknown creature went its own way, noisily, and was quickly swallowed by the dark woods. If our dog was frightened, it was just a little less so than were my brother and I. That evening, so the family tale goes, when it came time for bedtime stories, one of us youngsters said, "Daddy, will you tell us some Jesus stories?"

The experience reveals a common, fundamental yearning and inclination: humanity instinctively seeks its security in its religious orientation. Whether by "Jesus stories" or "Moses stories" or tales from some other religious orientation, people are comforted, sustained, and given hope by their religious faith.

In a time when individuals and nations are confronted by horrendous fears and seemingly unsolvable problems, it is appropriate to call to mind "some Jesus stories." It is difficult to imagine situations that do not yield to the promise and encouragement offered by the biblical faiths.

A world that is in dire need of hope in the midst of its largest fears could do worse than look to religious faith.

Listening for Life

It is difficult for us who sit in the relative safety of earthquake-free (at the moment) regions to imagine the terror, turmoil, and grief that has accompanied the recent tragedy in Mexico.

Among the images that remain from those agonized days are brief scenes from two television news reports. One is of a group of workers frantically searching for survivors in a toppled high-rise apartment building. Suddenly word comes that cries for help are thought to be heard from deep within the rubble.

The camera catches the drama. A supervisor calls for quiet—"*Silencio!*" The call is relayed quickly down the line and all activity stops while those closest to the sounds try to speak with the survivor.

Quickly the frantic efforts begin again and one

assumes a life soon may be saved.

The second image is similar. The camera zooms to a worker high atop the rubble of a destroyed building. The report comes that a child, trapped for three days, has been located but is in need of "encouragement." What the television viewer sees takes only a moment, but the impact is powerful: a dozen or so workers, picks and shovels resting for the moment, shout in unison to the unseen child to "hold on," that help is near.

Brief images, yes, but powerful in their symbolism—that when tragedy strikes and our fellow human beings are in peril, we join together and spare no energy to save the endangered.

Surely the larger lesson is not lost: that cries for help may be heard all around us these days, whether they be from teenagers who despair of the future and see little reason to live, or the grieving who have lost loved ones, or the ill who never are free from pain, or the elderly who have outlived lifelong friends and are strangers in an unfamiliar world, or the starving who appear more like walking skeletons, or the world's huddled masses yearning for release from the prison of world militarism.

The cry "Silence!" is always appropriate in this noise-filled, hell-bent-for-destruction world. Our planet sorely needs listeners who, having paused and heard, will join ranks to save their brothers and sisters in peril.

Hang on, world. A lot of people are digging.

In Quest of Good News

It's a comment frequently heard: "They don't print good news anymore." That such a remark isn't true doesn't diminish the feelings of frustration and anguish it reveals. People, these days, feel overwhelmed by events of the day—and many of those events are of a heavy, foreboding bad news nature.

But, again, what else is new? Almost every generation could have made such an observation about its own time. Hasn't it always been this way?

One is tempted by such thoughts to set out on a search for good news, not realizing that such a search is itself an acknowledgment of just how bad things are.

Nevertheless, occasional forays in quest of good news should not be condemned. Perhaps one may be forgiven for such lapses.

While too much could be made of each instance noted below (cases could be made to the contrary), we submit that the world is not totally bereft of good news. Witness the following:

■The world's collective conscience seems in good, perhaps even robust, health, as evidenced by such happenings as increased attention to peace movements and continuing sensitivity to human rights, ecological, and other issues.

■The world's capacity for moral outrage, though overburdened in recent times, remains intact. That man's inhumanity to man will not be lightly accepted is perhaps small cause for rejoicing—but it is, nevertheless, good news. People recognize wrong, they know immoral behavior—whether it's their own or someone else's—when they see it. That qualifies as good news.

■The healthy state of compassion and caring—the way empathy and sympathy are shared among human beings in the face of the world's problems—is a cause for encouragement. That there are people who care, who suffer when their fellow beings suffer, is good news.

■There are learned, wise men and women—scientists, educators, businessmen, clergy, students, and others—dedicated to finding a better way in this world. They realize the urgency of the issues and are not willing to surrender the future to humanity's selfishness, error, foolishness, and sin.

■There are strong communities of faith throughout the world, where prayer and good works and sacrificial deeds are practiced daily. These are places where the forgotten are remembered, where the powerless find support, where the unloved are loved, and where justice and mercy are pursued. Such communities are symbols of renewal and hope. They are the grandest lights that shine in a dark time.

For those who will look, good news may be found.

About My Operation

It's bad enough to have to go to the hospital, but it's worse to do so and have one of those operations that polite people don't talk about in mixed company. I did both. I went to the hospital about three weeks ago, and I had one of those kinds of operations.

Now, that's all you'll hear about the operation itself; however, it's necessary that I inflict upon you some other details of my recent medical history in order to make a point. I've never enjoyed reading this kind of stuff myself, so I'll understand if you choose to be excused at this point.

While the medical people were fiddlin' around with my insides, they discovered some rare and exotic disorder in one of my internal things and in the bone marrow in my sternum. Not good, they said. I agreed, as I had been experiencing some symptoms unrelated to the reason for my surgery.

They had some good news for me: the condition can be treated and overcome. There was some not-so-good news, too—the treatment, requiring a minimum of six weeks of daily hour-long intravenous medication, along with a big wad of ugly capsules, leaves one feeling somewhere down the scale below "yukky."

"Yes," my doctor said in response to my question, "when you've recovered, you'll be able to play the piano." (Doctors are nice to put up with such old jokes.)

Now, to the point. It's true what they say: those of us who have enjoyed good health have taken it for granted. I can't recall missing a day's work in decades because of illness and really don't know how to appreciate such a blessing. There are a lot of folks out there who suffer daily, over extended periods of time. In my book, these people are our real unsung heroes.

Illness brings a lot of things into perspective. It reminds us of our dependence upon others—of our inter-dependence, really. (There's a universal lesson in this. How much better our international relations would be if we tried to "bear one another's burdens" more than trying to better our position at others' expense. That may be too simplistic and idealistic, but it's worthy of pondering.)

Some reflections on my hospitalization may help make my point:

■I remember a young orderly, who, while wheeling me back to my room after some X-rays, talked excitedly of his work and his college training. After seeing me safe, he left with a simple parting that I must have heard and spoken thousands of times, but that had never, until that moment, contained such grace, peace, and love. "God bless you, sir!" is all he said.

■I remember the deeply moving prayer of a Catholic deacon; the skill and professionalism and personal care of my doctors and nurses; the visits and good words from friends in St. Vincent Infirmary's pastoral care department and contacts from numerous other friends—expressions that all conveyed more than was ever spoken or written.

■I remember that while I lay on my bed in my skimpy hospital gown, my pretty neighbor came in and, given an advantageous view of my skinny remains, remarked, "Hey, John, you've really got cute legs." That's good medicine.

■I remember the nice young lab technician, who, after taking a blood sample and chatting a while, pinched my big toe through the bedcovers as she left the room. They ought to train all hospital people to do that.

Enough of this. There's no particular moral here, unless one catches you along the way. Just remember: sick or well, you can find God's blessings everywhere. You really can have a nice day.

Blue Skies Remembered

In part of me that belongs more to yesterday than today, I remember blue skies. They are the skies of youth, when all skies were blue.

I remember, particularly, blue skies seen from the top of Mount Magazine, from where, as far as the eye could see, blue skies met green horizon and all the world was beautiful. Uncut forests stretched in all directions, relieved only by an occasional farm adorning a lush, fertile valley.

That was another time, another world.

Today, such pristine blue skies seem a rarity, freaks of a perverted nature playing tricks on an ever-encroaching pollution that sends acid rain to poison our lakes and trees, imperiling otherwise endangered species and casting a pall on the human heart and soul.

Today, from the mountaintop of my childhood memories, the horizon, when visible, is assaulted by once-proud forests now scarred with ugly remnants of clear-cut "harvesting," that benevolent phrase that man's greed has devised to excuse yet another rape of the land.

The businessmen-scientists have all kinds of arguments ready to convince me that clear-cutting is a wise, even benevolent practice. A bird, a squirrel, a fish, and a frightened young walnut tree who couldn't find her mother told me not to believe them.

Men have gone forth to subdue the earth, claiming license from a good Book.

Who are to be the friends of the earth these days?

Surely among that group must be people of faith, those commissioned to be good stewards of creation.

The mantle is not an easy one in a time when consumerism and greed and unbridled profit and perverted progress have wreaked terrible penalties on both the land and the human spirit.

The mantle means taking on some of society's most entrenched sacred cows. It involves nothing less than a wrenching, traumatic, radical review of values and lifestyles. Only people of faith—people who remember who they are and what the earth is—can furnish adequate motivation for such a task.

Will the skies ever be blue again?

We have to believe so. To not believe so is to give in, to surrender to the smog, to concede the victory to humanity's lower nature.

I have a dream. Someday my grandchildren's children will stand on the top of Mount Magazine and see blue skies and whole green forests and breathe clear mountain air and drink from pure, rushing streams.

Are old men fools?

Is Optimism an Option?

What does one do when overwhelmed with the temptation to say something positive, something nice and good and optimistic, about things in general these days?

Given at least one mood of the times, a likely reaction would be to resist stoutly such an inclination, confident that it, too, will pass, convinced that the old and dependable pessimisms are, after all, more appropriate to the times. As the sign says: "Anyone who can be optimistic in times like these just doesn't understand what's going on."

The thought poses a question: is it being honest—is it even *possible*—to be an authentically positive and optimistic person these days? Considering the ominous forebodings and dire predictions that bombard our times, is optimism really an option for the '80s?

Even to ask the question, some would say, reflects the extent to which negativism has won the day. However, when asked from the faith perspective, the question reveals some hidden gems, some grand surprises, that the biblical religions hold in store for difficult days.

One of those priceless gems is hope. The biblical word for hope is not one to be used casually or glibly. Biblical hope is more than superficial wishing and shallow optimism. It is not the desperation of a coward. Just as the Bible offers no cheap grace, neither does it promise a hope trivialized by the popular understandings of the word.

Biblical hope is bound up with, and inseparable from, faith. It involves assurances and convictions that, rather than being presumptuous, are humble confessions of the sovereignty of God. Scriptural hope acknowledges a dependency on God that human self-sufficiency rejects.

Biblical hope is active, not passive. It is a way of living.

It is an involvement in the present and a stance toward the future that reflect a shared responsibility for God's creation.

All of the above is to say that one of the most positive, good things that can be observed about our times is that there are people of hope scattered throughout the world. Given the particular nature and talents of different individuals, this hope is expressed in a variety of ways: from quiet faithfulness in daily prayer to a stubborn persistence in front-line fighting for human rights; from spending long hours strengthening family life to crusading on behalf of the poor and the imprisoned and the powerless; from the more pastoral comforting and sustaining ministries to the prophetic witness of laying down one's life as a witness for peace—perhaps, even, in some grand act of moral obedience (what society calls civil disobedience).

The good news is that these many and varied expressions of hope are being "lived out" daily around us. They give us quiet assurance and joy. They remind us that for people of the biblical faiths, hope and optimism are not options. They are responsibilities.

Members of the Funeral

I attended two funeral services this week, and the experience caused me to think about those things that death cannot take from us.

It isn't true, of course, that death does not deprive us. It most certainly does. Death's sting is a very real and grievous one. Nothing in the Judeo-Christian funeral service should ever suggest that the loss of loved ones isn't a traumatic experience.

But it remains that there are things that death cannot

ultimately capture. Though it is never pleasant to think about death, it is helpful to consider those realities that resist its seeming finality.

■Death cannot take away the love that parents, children, family members, and friends have for their deceased loved one. Such love remains. It survives the apparent final victory of the grave.

■Death cannot take away the contribution a person has made, no matter how briefly or how long that person may have lived. Death cannot erase the beauty of the life, the dreams dreamed, the love given and received, the good done, the hopes and plans nurtured. Such realities remain, immune to the finalities of physical death.

■Death cannot take away the ultimate commitment to life that is the gift of those who remain. That commitment is perhaps the greatest honor that can be paid to the deceased—for the surviving to take up life and live it with vigor and joy and purpose, to keep on keeping on. Such a response is perhaps the grandest memorial a deceased loved one could receive.

While participating in a funeral service, among friends of years past and strangers whom one does not know, one is reminded that death is the great common denominator. It is the ultimate reality that sooner or later will be the lot of all beings. Riches, fame, achievement, and whatever status society may bestow do not exempt one from the grim reaper's ultimate harvest. Death is the final arbiter. We are all peers before death. We are all members of the funeral.

A funeral service is an occasion to ponder life's mysteries, to think about values, to reflect on meanings, to wonder about the mystery of life.

There is a sense in which time is both enemy and friend. It is enemy in that it steals our days, our years, and finally our physical lives. It is friend in that it enriches those same days and years, that it heals our wounds and covers those scars we may have inflicted by our own thoughtlessness, error, or sin.

If time doesn't remove those causes for remorse, it at least graciously softens their pain.

A funeral service enables us to say with Scripture and ancient ritual that which our words by themselves are inadequate to express. Surrounded by the symbols of faith, we are reminded of causes that are worthy of the highest commitment and the ultimate sacrifice.

Death, viewed from the eyes of faith, does not lose its pain. It does, however, lose its ultimate victory.

A Good Question

The question came from a friend, a respected worker for peace and human betterment for half a century. "There's something I need to ask you," he said. "What reasons for hope do you have?"

The question is one of those stoppers, the kind that causes one to pause and respond, "That's really a good question."

The inquiry came following Tuesday's awards banquet at which thirteen Arkansans were honored by the Arkansas Peace Center as "senior peacemakers." The thirteen, all 65 years or older, were recognized for their contributions—often in quiet, sacrificial ways—to the cause of peace.

The evening was a good one, a warming one, an encouraging one. It both honored and inspired the kind of idealism associated with such a noble cause as world peace.

The question, from one of the honorees, was disarmingly honest though eminently appropriate: what, indeed, are humanity's reasons for hope in a time when 50,000 nuclear weapons hang over the human race by a thin thread of trust and chance? What hope for survival is there in such a time as this?

It is, in fact, a good question, that goes to the heart of the human condition. It's a question for all seasons. People of faith always should be ready to give an account of the hope that is within them.

What reasons for hope? I have some answers for my friend.

■"People like you," I told my friend, "are one of my reasons for hope." It was an honest response, with no intention of being patronizing. People of good will and unfailing dedication to the cause of peace are one of the authentic, visible reasons for hope in this world. They are a force that evil has not yet been able to overcome.

■A swelling tide, worldwide, of concern for peace. General Dwight Eisenhower said it: someday the world's citizens will rise up in such strength to demand peace that their leaders will have to give it to them.

■A renewed awareness of the oneness of the human family and of the absolute necessity of peace within that family.

Once the Apostle Paul, after three days in a violent storm at sea, declared, "All hope of our being saved was at last abandoned .... So we cast out three anchors into the storm."

Hope is always a firm anchor in a storm.

Persons who have hope are our strength. We call them peacemakers. The Bible calls them blessed.

Report from "Away"

Four days after Christmas I entered the hospital and on the second day of the new year learned I had cancer.

Have a nice year.

I fully intend to. I will. I am.

I never liked to read "about my illness" pieces, and even less to write them. What follows is not my favorite indoor sport. But perhaps these lines will serve to inform the curious just what "away" their paper's religion writer has been to, as reported weekly on this page: "John Workman [after eight years I've given up trying to get our copy editors to always include my middle initial] is away. His column will resume when he returns."

So herewith a brief returning and resuming.

The current away from which I've temporarily returned is Houston, Texas, where I spent a couple of weeks undergoing tests and chemotherapy at M.D. Anderson Hospital and Tumor Institute, the central component of The University of Texas System Cancer Center. I am to return to Houston in about a week for surgery.

In order to tell this tale adequately, it now becomes necessary for you to learn more about my insides than you want to know—and certainly more than discreet Southerners like to tell about themselves.

I have leimyosarcoma, a rare type of cancer, centered in the pelvic region. According to the written report of one examining surgeon, who must have minored in creative writing, my tumor, a dandy, is "approaching volleyball size."

By such state-of-the-art terminology I suppose my surgery will be called a "slamdunkectomy."

A reflection, now. I have learned that one doesn't quickly adjust to the news of having cancer. I suppose such reluctance to accept reality is common regarding those events that have the potential to change one's life radically. We like to think we are in control of our lives.

There have been some long hours, enough discomfort, sufficient pain, and, early on, some tears.

It is interesting about the tears. As I suspect most people who have had similar experiences have learned, the tears are not so much for one's self, one's own plight and prospects. The tears are triggered by quite other factors—by the love being shown by family and friends, by the tender, stout compassion of skilled and dedicated physicians and medical experts. I've always known it: love, far more than fear of pain, is the mother of tears.

But all is not gloomy at such times. Consider at least one happy thing that happens when you know you're going to be examined by so many curious strangers: you get to buy new underwear.

Another bright thing: last Sunday, by radio, I heard my pastor remind me that according to Jeremiah, the same God that scattered God's people also will gather them. That was good news. I've been scattered and I'm standing in the need of being gathered.

And oh, yes ... It's good they're using my regular photo with this column and not my current likeness. Being forewarned that chemotherapy would cause what little hair I had to come out, I had my head shaved. One cheerful nurse, a prophet, told me that not only would my "regular" hair return but that "all that other hair you used to have on top" might also come back.

If that must be so, let God's will be done.

A closing thought. While being wheelchaired from the barber shop at that marvelous center of healing at Houston, I moved among scores of other hairless men, women, and children, many wearing the little telltale caps knitted by volunteers as love gifts. Although I had known for several weeks that I did, in fact, have cancer, that hallway experience became my confirmation rite, my full initiation into a very special fraternity.

I wasn't prepared for the impact of the experience. I

noticed that eyes that before had avoided my hesitant attempts at communication now sought me out. As glances were exchanged, unspoken but powerful greetings passed, silent signals of understanding, secret messages of shared healing and love. It was an over-whelmingly emotional experience, leaving me strangely empty yet full, drained yet buoyed.

I only hope my new companions didn't misunder-stand my tears, which were more of profound discovery than of regret or sorrow.

We, the hairless or otherwise marked of the world's cancer hospitals and homes, we who are being healed, would greet the rest of you with such messages. We've had the experience of being reminded, in a special way, that God wants nothing more than to heal this beautiful, though too-often fractured, world.

One More Report

Okay, let's get this over with because the one thing this column will not become is a continuing "About My Illness" saga.

It does seem appropriate, however, that a bit of updating is in order since my earlier report that I had cancer. I reported that I had been hospitalized at M.D. Anderson Hospital at Houston, had received chemotherapy, and would go back to Houston for surgery in mid-February. I have recently returned from that three-week stay.

In order to make sense of this, it again becomes neces-sary, as in my earlier column, that I undertake the un-pleasant task of telling you more than you want to know and more than I feel comfortable telling.

At Houston, the doctors removed a tumor originally

estimated as "approaching volleyball size" but which, after surgery, they described as "more of basketball size." The operation required the removal of my bladder and prostate gland and the construction of a urinary diversion. I was told that the latter device had enabled great numbers of patients to resume their former work, and even sports activities.

Although the doctors reported a very successful removal of the tumor, they recommended an extensive course of radiation treatments and chemotherapy at intervals over the next several months. During this time I expect to resume my work.

Now some comment.

As stated in the earlier column, I continue to learn that one doesn't quickly or easily adjust to having cancer and to the possible major changes that fact may mean for one's life. Nor is it easy to overcome the physical and emotional trauma of what my doctors called "about as major surgery as one can have."

But a happy note: I have accomplished (even exceeded), in record time, the weight loss program my family physician recommended several months ago. I lost about 37 pounds during this ordeal. Although I am slowly regaining some now-needed pounds, I am still startled by my own reflection in mirrors—sunken eyes staring from a gaunt face and a seemingly-shrunken head highlighted by the chemotherapy-induced loss of what little hair I had. But all this, too, will pass.

It would be nice if I could report to you that I have been a pillar of strength through all of this, but that would be a less-than-honest report. Although returning strength brings more positive thoughts daily, the truth is that I have experienced, as never before, overwhelming fears, a suffocating uncertainty about the future, and to me perhaps most unsettling of all, what I can only confess as a weakness of spiritual strength.

It helped little to try to tell myself that such thoughts were to be expected following major surgery. The fears, embarrassingly selfish and perhaps highly unrealistic, persisted. What would happen if my wife, on whom I was so increasingly dependent, should become ill? What of my financial security, including provision for future medical care, if I could no longer be employed? What if the cancer returned and I faced more, perhaps even worse, terrors than those of these dark days?

Although our recent lovely pre-spring weather and my returning strength are putting such thoughts in perspective, I cannot deny that they were my principal agenda during a couple of weeks of restless days and sleepless nights.

But hang on—there's an "up side" to all this.

I have received new insights into some basic lessons of life. I know now that it's human amid such circumstances to believe that one's faith is weak. I have a new appreciation of the biblical reminder that when we are weak, then we are strong because we are compelled to depend more on God.

I have been reminded of the great comfort and strength that come from the love and support of family and friends. (I wish I could personally respond to the scores of cards, letters, and telephone calls that have come from readers of this column, contacts that have meant so very much to me.)

I have learned how grand a library the mind is in time of trial, how the exercise of both memory and anticipation can help with one's healing.

I have learned that humor not only dies hard but must have at least nine lives. They took out a bunch of my insides, but I am discovering more each day that, happily, they missed my funnybone. Thank God for that.

Enough now. With this we say farewell to public talk of my illness. Consider yourself lucky.

Life is sweet. Spring is at hand. Lent brings renewal. God is good and gratitude remains the grandest life-stance of all.

On with the show!

The Dragon Slayers

It's been with me as long as I can remember, a part of my personal baggage since childhood: the haunting prospect that some day, in some faraway place, I would be confronted with the challenge to survive.

The thought, although not an obsession, has been part of my style—reflected when packing for Boy Scout trips as a youth and later as a scoutmaster (what if we should become stranded?); when preparing for overseas trips (take these pliers, this bit of wire, this knife, because you could need them to get out of that foreign prison); and when backpacking in Colorado or bicycle camping in Arkansas (you never know when you might be kidnapped by wild bears, now do you?).

In moderation, that kind of thinking needn't be all bad. It at least adds to the fun of the adventure.

As envisioned when I was a youngster, my personal battle to survive might come after my 35-foot ketch, on which I was sailing singlehanded around the world, was washed ashore on a coral reef in the South Pacific.

Or when my open-cockpit biplane, during one of my many record-setting flights to the unexplored regions of the world, ran out of fuel over Africa's Kalahari Desert.

Or perhaps when I was hiking alone across Outer Mongolia, making my way south, through hordes of bandits, to the high Himalayas to become the first Razorback ever to make such a daring trans-continental trek—plus climbing solo to the top of Mount Everest (by the never-conquered North Wall).

But wherever and whenever, I always have believed the day would come when I would, at last, have my shot at the challenge to survive. As a youth, I knew I would be up to it.

I now have been given that challenge.

It has not come, however, as I had dreamed and certainly not as I would have chosen.

My challenge is not without some of the elements I had imagined—danger, fear, uncertainty, and no small portion of suffering.

Though in a far land, my challenge has a name not found on any map.

It is cancer.

Twice on this page I have broken my vow not to write about my illness. But I owe a debt to some of you out there—to you who know, more keenly than I, what this challenge to survive is all about. I need to thank you for the help your stalwart example has been to me.

To date, my personal battle has involved chemotherapy, surgery, and six weeks of radiation. In response to a doctor at Houston who told me I must now undergo a ten-month session of chemotherapy, I began to counter with all the reasons I'd just as soon pass, if it was okay with him.

As if to say he really hadn't gotten my attention, the doctor replied, "Look. You're fighting a dragon here. It can kill you deader than dead."

He got my attention. I spent last week in a hospital, beginning the next stage in what I now have taken some comfort in thinking of as my long-anticipated, even strangely longed-for (does that sound too perverse?) "challenge to survive."

So this is it, I thought. "You're fighting a dragon here." But for most of my life I've been preparing to fight dragons—whether in Outer Mongolia, the high Himalayas, the South Pacific, or along Arkansas's mountain trails and roads.

And I've known some dragon slayers in my time. They've fought fiercely against all kinds of odds, sometimes even doing the dragons in.

It's from those dear people—the slayers of the dragons of illness, fear, personal problems, loss, grief—that I now take great courage.

They've shown me how to pull the sword from the rock.

Bring on the dragons. My kit bag is full, the sun is at my back, and I'm on the high ground.

"There Are Lions Out There!"

I have a friend who tells a delightful story about lions in Africa. I first heard the account, and tape-recorded it, some half-dozen years ago while a guest in my friend's home in Morogoro, Tanzania, in eastern Africa. Since then the tale has become a favorite, replayed numerous times for family and friends.

The account, heard in anticipation of my own first sightings of wild animals on the vast African plains, was enhanced by the setting. Following a grand late evening meal, enjoyed by myself and two friends with whom I was traveling, our host, an American teacher, told the lion story as one of several in response to our request to "tell us some tales about life in Africa." I can vividly recall the scene, even these years later, as the sounds of the warm African night winds, stirring leaves on trees outside the house, are heard on the recording.

My friend tells how he and an associate were touring in East Africa with the associate's father, who was visiting from the States. One evening they decided to camp in a game park. Asking an official if it was safe to sleep in the open, the reply was, "Yes, but it would be better if you stayed in this border post hut." When asked why, the official replied, "Because there are lions out there."

My friend recalled that he and his associates were "brave Americans who'd been on a lion safari and had slept out in lion country before." But to be reassured, he asked the official, "Will the lions bother us?" The answer was to the effect of "No—but they're out there."

To shorten the story—which is to rob you of the joy of

174

hearing it as told—the three decided to camp out under the stars. Before going to sleep, they gathered wood and built a big fire ("wild animals don't like fires, you know") and set up a "lion alarm system"—a string with tin cans attached ("so they would tink, tink, tink if a lion touched them").

The three had been asleep only a short time, my friend recounted, when suddenly the quiet night air was rent by the awesome roar of a lion, coming from just a few yards in front of them.

"If you've never heard the roar of a lion at night ... well, there's just nothing like it. It literally shook the ground .... We were in that car so fast you couldn't believe it!"

After about an hour, my friend, feeling cramped in the small Volkswagen "beetle," assumed the lions had gone their way. He opted for more sleeping room outside.

He got out and arranged his sleeping bag on the ground. Wanting to make one final check on his lion alarm system, he turned on the car lights. His excited, animated report: "Right there, just six feet in front of me, were two of the biggest lions I'd ever seen!"

He spent the rest of the night in the car.

I've often wondered about the appeal of that story, now known in our family as "the lion story." The account was told with no moral in mind, and it isn't fair to rob such grand stories of their own inherent beauty by forcing morals on them. But perhaps one lesson may be drawn.

Most of the things we fear never really come to pass. Most of the things we worry about never happen. Most of those things we dread never materialize. Most of our lions in the dark never bother us.

There are, to be sure, lions out there these days. And often the wisest course is to sleep in the car. But too much caution can cause one to miss the marvelous beauties of the night.

About the Author

A fifth-generation Methodist clergyman, John S. Workman was educated at Hendrix College in Conway, Arkansas, and Perkins School of Theology in Dallas, Texas. After serving in the U.S. Army Security Agency in Japan and Korea, he served churches in Oil Trough, Sylvan Hills, Berryville, Cabot, and Little Rock, Arkansas. As a writer, he has traveled to Africa, Europe, and Central America pursuing stories of interest to the religious press. His works have appeared in *New World Outlook*, *A.D. Magazine*, *The Circuit Rider*, and other publications. Formerly editor of the *Arkansas Methodist* newspaper, he is currently Religion Editor of the *Arkansas Gazette*.

About the Editor

Sally Crisp has been the director of the Writing Center at the University of Arkansas at Little Rock since 1981 and has taught writing at the college level since 1972. She lives in Little Rock with her husband and two daughters.